Children in Families Under Stress

Anna-Beth Doyle, Dolores Gold,
Debbie S. Moskowitz, *Editors*

NEW DIRECTIONS FOR CHILD DEVELOPMENT
WILLIAM DAMON, *Editor-in-Chief*

Number 24, June 1984

Paperback sourcebooks in
The Jossey-Bass Social and Behavioral Sciences Series

Jossey-Bass Inc., Publishers
San Francisco • Washington • London

Anna-Beth Doyle, Dolores Gold, Debbie S. Moskowitz (Eds.).
Children in Families Under Stress.
New Directions for Child Development, no. 24.
San Francisco: Jossey-Bass, 1984.

New Directions for Child Development Series
William Damon, *Editor-in-Chief*

New Directions for Child Development (publication number
USPS 494-090) is published quarterly by Jossey-Bass Inc., Publishers.
Second-class postage rates are paid at San Francisco, California,
and at additional mailing offices.

Correspondence:
Subscriptions, single-issue orders, change of address notices, undelivered
copies, and other correspondence should be sent to Subscriptions,
Jossey-Bass Inc., Publishers, 433 California Street, San Francisco
California 94104.

Editorial correspondence should be sent to the Editor-in-Chief,
William Damon, Department of Psychology, Clark University,
Worcester, Massachusetts 01610.

Library of Congress Catalogue Card Number LC 83-82717
International Standard Serial Number ISSN 0195-2269
International Standard Book Number ISBN 87589-984-6

Cover art by Willi Baum
Manufactured in the United States of America

Ordering Information

The paperback sourcebooks listed below are published quarterly and can be ordered either by subscription or single-copy.

Subscriptions cost $35.00 per year for institutions, agencies, and libraries. Individuals can subscribe at the special rate of $25.00 per year *if payment is by personal check.* (Note that the full rate of $35.00 applies if payment is by institutional check, even if the subscription is designated for an individual.) Standing orders are accepted. Subscriptions normally begin with the first of the four sourcebooks in the current publication year of the series. When ordering, please indicate if you prefer your subscription to begin with the first issue of the *coming* year.

Single copies are available at $8.95 when payment accompanies order, and *all single-copy orders under $25.00 must include payment.* (California, New Jersey, New York, and Washington, D.C., residents please include appropriate sales tax.) For billed orders, cost per copy is $8.95 plus postage and handling. (Prices subject to change without notice.)

Bulk orders (ten or more copies) of any individual sourcebook are available at the following discounted prices: 10–49 copies, $8.05 each; 50–100 copies, $7.15 each; over 100 copies, *inquire.* Sales tax and postage and handling charges apply as for single copy orders.

To ensure correct and prompt delivery, all orders must give either the *name of an individual* or an *official purchase order number.* Please submit your order as follows:

Subscriptions: specify series and year subscription is to begin.
Single Copies: specify sourcebook code (such as, CD8) and first two words of title.

Mail orders for United States and Possessions, Latin America, Canada, Japan, Australia, and New Zealand to:
Jossey-Bass Inc., Publishers
433 California Street
San Francisco, California 94104

Mail orders for all other parts of the world to:
Jossey-Bass Limited
28 Banner Street
London EC1Y 8QE

New Directions for Child Development Series
William Damon, *Editor-in-Chief*

CD1   *Social Cognition,* William Damon
CD2   *Moral Development,* William Damon
CD3   *Early Symbolization,* Howard Gardner, Dennie Wolf
CD4   *Social Interaction and Communication During Infancy,* Ina C. Uzgiris
CD5   *Intellectual Development Beyond Childhood,* Deanna Kuhn
CD6   *Fact, Fiction, and Fantasy in Childhood,* Ellen Winner, Howard Gardner

CD7   *Clinical-Developmental Psychology,* Robert L. Selman, Regina Yando
CD8   *Anthropological Perspectives on Child Development,* Charles M. Super,
      Sara Harkness
CD9   *Children's Play,* Kenneth H. Rubin
CD10 *Children's Memory,* Marion Perlmutter
CD11 *Developmental Perspectives on Child Maltreatment,* Ross Rizley, Dante Cicchetti
CD12 *Cognitive Development,* Kurt W. Fischer
CD13 *Viewing Children Through Television,* Hope Kelly, Howard Gardner
CD14 *Childrens' Conceptions of Health, Illness, and Bodily Functions,*
      Roger Bibace, Mary E. Walsh
CD15 *Children's Conceptions of Spatial Relationships,* Robert Cohen
CD16 *Emotional Development,* Dante Cicchetti, Petra Hesse
CD17 *Developmental Approaches to Giftedness and Creativity,*
      David Henry Feldman
CD18 *Children's Planning Strategies,* David Forbes, Mark T. Greenberg
CD19 *Children and Divorce,* Lawrence A. Kurdek
CD20 *Child Development and International Development: Research-Policy Interfaces,*
      Daniel A. Wagner
CD21 *Levels and Transitions in Children's Development,* Kurt W. Fischer
CD22 *Adolescent Development in the Family,* Harold D. Grotevant,
      Catherine R. Cooper
CD23 *Children's Learning in the "Zone of Proximal Development,"*
      Barbara Rogoff, James V. Wertsch

Contents

Editors' Notes   **1**
Anna-Beth Doyle, Dolores Gold, Debbie S. Moskowitz

Part 1. The Effects of Marital Discord, Divorce, and Parental Psychopathology

Chapter 1. Stress and Coping in Children and Families   **7**
E. Mavis Hetherington
The literature on child development in families under stress is examined in
relation to the concepts and methods of stress research.

Chapter 2. Marital Discord and Children: **35**
Problems, Strategies, Methodologies, and Results
K. Daniel O'Leary
The development of children whose parents are in conflict with each other is
reviewed with an emphasis on methodology.

Chapter 3. Family Affect and Communication Related to Schizophrenia   **47**
Michael J. Goldstein
A series of studies investigating the influence of family interactions on the
development of schizophrenia is described.

Part 2. The Effects of an Atypical Child on Family Functioning

Chapter 4. Families with Problem Children   **65**
Eric J. Mash
A focus on conceptual issues in the context of families functioning with an
atypical child is provided.

Chapter 5. Social Interactions: A Transactional Approach with   **85**
Illustrations from Children with Developmental Problems
Linda S. Siegel, Charles E. Cunningham
A transactional approach is used to explore child–adult interactions.

Chapter 6. Current Adjustment and Family Functioning of Children   **99**
Behaviorally at Risk for Adult Schizophrenia
Jane E. Ledingham, Alex E. Schwartzman, Lisa A. Serbin
The functioning of children who are regarded as deviant by their peers is
examined at home and in the school.

Index   **113**

Editors' Notes

This sourcebook presents an overview of the complex concepts and methodologies in current research on children in troubled families. In early research on the family context and child development, the mother-child dyad was predominantly studied in isolation. Later, the dyad became a triad including the father, and recently interest in the effects of siblings on each other has increased. Paralleling this elaboration of family variables, there has been a recognition of the importance of the social context of families. Originally, social context was conceptualized unidimensionally, referring solely to socioeconomic status of a family. However, researchers have since recognized the importance of other social variables in family functioning—for example, the effects of maternal employment status, single parenting, and the quality of the neighborhood. Researchers on children in families have also become more sophisticated in their conceptualization of the direction of effects. Emphasis has changed from unidirectional models of parents' effects on children to reciprocal models of the effects of the child and family on each other. Moreover, current models not only examine first-order effects of the influence of one family member on another but also the second-order (rippling) effects of this influence on other family members.

This greater elaboration of models for the study of families should lead to more accurate prediction of the parameters involved in problems affecting individual development and family functioning. However, greater specificity can lead to fragmentation in what variables are under study, and can hinder the development of conceptual interconnections among diverse research programs. The concept of stress has the potential to organize the threads that connect several areas of family research. This concept has been productively applied to many fields in the behavioral sciences, at multiple levels of analysis—for example, to cultures, communities, small groups, and individuals. This sourcebook brings together research that examines the implications of stress for families in two theme areas: in families with an atypical family member, and in those experiencing marital discord and divorce. These two themes initially appear different but have structural similarities when examined from the perspective of models of stress.

At the most general level, stress has been defined as an inability to respond to external pressure. Thus, stress can be considered the outcome of a discrepancy between external events and response capabilities. The chapters that follow vary in their focus as to who in the family creates stress for the other members and by whom the consequences of stress are experienced. In Part One, stressors are defined primarily in terms of parental characteristics. Mavis Hetherington (Chapter One) provides an overview of research on stress

1

2

and families from this perspective. She reviews types of stress; conceptual models of stress from psychology, sociology, and life cycle theory; and the strengths and weaknesses of methods derived from these different models with particular reference to studies of divorce. In Chapter Two, Daniel O'Leary focuses on marital discord and the consequent behavior problems in children. According to both authors, the major characteristic of children that mitigates the severity of outcome is gender; that is, boys appear to be more vulnerable to the stressor of marital discord. In Chapter Three, Michael Goldstein presents a detailed analysis of parental communication and emotional styles, showing that parents with a high level of communication deviance, in combination with emotional overinvolvement with their children or frequent criticism of them, have offspring who are at greater risk for developing schizophrenia.

Stressors can also be related to the characteristics of the child. In Part Two, Eric Mash (Chapter Four) describes how children, for example hyperactive children, may be stressors; and how the consequences of such a stressor may be observed in the parents, with outcomes such as marital conflict and parental mood disturbance. Mash avoids an oversimplification of the potential direction of effects and reviews evidence on parental attitudes, expectations, and control techniques as antecedents as well as consequents of problem behaviors in children. Linda Siegal and Charles Cunningham (Chapter Five) illustrate this approach by focusing on problem children—specifically, children who are premature or developmentally delayed. They recognize the response capacities of the parents in terms of ability or inability to provide attention and stimulation to such a child, which causes further delay in the child's development. In Chapter Six, Jane Ledingham, Alex Schwartzman, and Lisa Serbin describe an ongoing longitudinal study in which several types of behavioral childhood deviance are examined. One aspect of this work is a study of the influence of a deviant child on the family's organization and functioning.

This sourcebook is the result of an interdisciplinary conference sponsored by the Centre for Research in Human Development (CRDH) at Concordia University in Montreal, Canada, and supported by the Social Sciences and Humanities Research Council of Canada and Le Programme de Formation de Chercheurs et d'Action Concertée of Quebec. The chapters in this book are based on the major addresses given at that conference. Many other people participated in the conference both in formal presentations and in informal discussions. We regret that space and time limitations did not permit us to represent their ideas and projects here. Several individuals deserve special recognition for their contributions to the organization of that conference: Lisa Serbin, director of the Centre for Research in Human Development; Alex Schwartzman and Donna White, members of the conference planning board; and Helen Raicevic, coordinator of CRDH, who set up local arrangements for the conference and helped bring this book to completion.

Anna-Beth Doyle
Dolores Gold
Debbie S. Moskowitz

Anna-Beth Doyle is associate professor of psychology and member of the Centre for Research in Human Development at Concordia University in Montreal, Canada. Her research in the area of social development has focused on childrearing environments and peer relations.

Dolores Gold is professor of psychology and a member of the Centre for Research in Human Development at Concordia University. She has performed research examining the socialization of children and is presently studying the psychological development of the elderly.

Debbie S. Moskowitz is assistant professor of psychology at McGill University and associate member of the Centre for Research in Human Development at Concordia University. She has been a National Science Foundation National Needs Fellow and has published in the areas of personality theory, assessment, and development.

.

PART 1.

The Effects of Marital Discord, Divorce, and Parental Psychopathology

This chapter reviews issues in theory and methodology in the study of stress and coping in children and families.

Stress and Coping in Children and Families

E. Mavis Hetherington

Members of contemporary society have become increasingly aware of stress and its consequences. Adults, adolescents, and even children discuss the destruction of the environment, the possibility of nuclear war, the depletion of natural resources, the disposal of hazardous wastes, and the presence of food additives and carcinogens as a routine part of everyday life. Parents and children are aware that the family is changing, divorce is frequent, remarriage is not unlikely, and a family in which both parents work may be essential in dealing with the rising cost of living. Adolescents discuss with equanimity the problems of drug abuse and alcoholism, teen-aged pregnancy, and the epidemic of veneral disease. In addition, mass media and television have accustomed people to viewing scenes of war, violence, destruction, atrocities, carnage, and mutilation.

An interest in how people cope with such stressors has accompanied the increased awareness of and growing research literature on trauma in the lives of parents and children. Journals are replete with studies of responses to the birth of a sibling, loss of a parent through death or divorce, unemployment, the empty nest, retirement, and the impact of mental or physical illness on family functioning. This examination of the effects of stressful life events has yielded examples of successful and unsuccessful adaptations in children and families. Some children and families are permanently damaged by stressful life

A. Doyle, D. Gold, D. S. Moskowitz (Eds.). *Children in Families Under Stress.*
New Directions for Child Development, no. 24. San Francisco: Jossey-Bass, June 1984.

8

experiences; others go through turbulent transitions and emerge able to function competently or even with enhanced ability following their tribulations. This chapter begins with a discussion of some of the problems encountered in defining stress. It then reviews the theoretical and research traditions associated with the study of stress and coping in children and families. Finally, some of the factors that seem to mediate the experience of stress and successful or unsuccessful adaptive responses by children and families will be presented. Although the examples are drawn from a wide sample of the research literature on stress and coping, many are taken from research on family transitions, divorce, one-parent families, and remarriage.

Stress: Problems of Definition

In addressing the topic of stress and coping in children and families the first problem encountered is definitional. Although there is a persistent and widespread use of the terms *stress* and *coping* in the behavioral sciences, medicine, and psychiatry, there is little agreement about their meaning. This definitional confusion is reflected in Selye's (1980) recent introduction to a series of publications dealing with stress research. Selye asks,

> What is stress? Nowadays everyone seems to be talking about stress. You have it not only in daily conversation but also through television, radio, the newspapers, and the constantly increasing number of conferences, stress centers and university courses that are devoted to the topic. Yet remarkably few people define the concept the same way or even bother to attempt a clear-cut definition. The businessman thinks of it as frustration or emotional tension, the air traffic controller as a problem in concentration, the biochemist and endocrinologist as a purely chemical event, the athlete as muscular tension. This list could be extended to almost every human experience or activity, and, somewhat surprisingly, most people. . . think of their own occupations as being the most stressful. Similarly, most of us believe that ours is "the age of stress," forgetting that the caveman's fear of being attacked by wild animals while he slept, or dying from hunger, cold or exhaustion, must have been just as stressful as our fear of a world war, the crash of the stock exchange, overpopulation, or the unpredictability of the future.
> Somewhat ironically, there is a grain of truth in every formulation of stress because all demands upon our adaptability do evoke the stress phenomenon (p. 7).

Stress has been defined both in terms of stimulus and response characteristics. For example, stress can be described as a stimulus or force that, if sufficiently strong, can produce strain in the person encountering it. Note that this definition includes the strength of the stimulus that affects the individual and the strain produced by the stimulus. This strain is likely to be reflected in chemical and psychophysiological reactions and in changes in psychological or emotional state. Stress has also been defined as a broad interactive network of factors that include stimulus, response, individual characteristics, evaluations, and coping styles. Whatever definition is used, most scientists would agree that stress activates individuals to modify or adapt to their situation and that this adaptation, which we call *coping*, can be either successful or unsuccessful.

To understand outcomes of stress and coping, they cannot be viewed solely in terms of the properties of the stressful events. They must be considered in terms of personal or family history, individual or family characteristics and resources, the social and physical context, and the interpretation or appraisal of the event. The interplay among these factors and their impact may change over time and vary for different family members. There can be no clear identification of events as stressful or nonstressful since experiencing an event as stressful depends on a complex interaction between the individual and the environment.

Dimensions of Stressful Events

Many attempts have been made to identify the salient dimensions of stressful events. These events have been differentiated from nonstressful events in terms of their temporal pattern, intensity, affective quality, and frequency.

Some events, although extremely unpleasant at the time, have no long-term consequences. One might think of a parent searching for a young child who has wandered away from home as this type of circumscribed stressful event. Others are more prolonged but again time-limited, such as a serious illness. Some are continuous, such as the day-to-day conflicts in an unhappy marriage. Still other events involve long-term transactional effects. The transactional effects of a stressful event refer to an increase in the probability that a series of other stressors will follow the occurrence of a given stressful event.

Using teenaged pregnancies as an example of a stressful event, we find that women who have their first child as teenagers tend to drop out of school or marry younger and do not subsequently catch up educationally. In addition, young mothers have more children over time and this in turn limits their freedom to work. This lack of education, work skills, and available work time tends to be associated with poverty and a dependence on public assistance. Furstenberg (1976) found that one third of his sample of teenage mothers were on welfare, while only 4 percent of their peers were. In the United States it is estimated that well over half of all Aid for Dependent Children payments go to mothers who had their first child as a teenager. Thus, teenaged pregnancy initiates a cycle of low educational attainment, economic dependence, and poverty, and represents an event with long-term transactional effects.

Exits and Entrances. Another way in which life events have been differentiated is in terms of "exits" and "entrances" (Paykel, 1974). Exits include such things as death of a parent or the departure of the last child from the home. Entrances include the birth of a sibling or the addition of a step-parent. Although it has been argued that exits are more stressful for adults than entrances and are more closely associated with psychiatric disorder (Paykel, 1974), this finding seems to be largely attributable to the exits caused by death of a spouse and divorce — consistently rated as the two most stressful life event in general. Even then the perspective of the individual under study is important. It is unlikely that the death of an obnoxious, abusive, wealthy spouse in a conflict-ridden marriage necessarily will be viewed as stressful.

In a similar way, some entrances such as the birth of a sibling may prove to be extremely stressful. Dunn and Kendrick (1980) found that following the birth of a sibling many first-born children tend to show emotional and behavioral problems. These problems are related to the temperament of the child and the emotional state of the mother, with children of depressed mothers showing more difficulties, and seem to be mediated to a large extent by changes in mother–child interaction. Mothers tend to become more negative, coercive, and restraining and to engage in less playful interactions with first-born children following the birth of a second child. Perhaps the birth of a sibling could be viewed as either the exit of maternal indulgence and attention or as the entrance of a sibling.

Affect and Stress. Can pleasant as well as unpleasant life changes be viewed as stressors that may be related to later disorders? Will a series of changes such as moving into a better job, a more pleasant neighborhood, or getting married be related to later psychological problems? There seems to be strong evidence that adverse outcomes are largely the result of unpleasant life changes. Even a series of significant life changes do not have lasting negative effects if they are pleasurable in quality.

Multiple Stressors. Another issue is whether a single stressful event has any prolonged harmful outcome. Rutter (1979a) has reported that when children experience only a single stress it carries no appreciable risk. However, when children are exposed to a series of stresses or several concurrent stresses the adverse effects increase multiplicatively, not as an additive function of the number of stresses. Even this seems to be an oversimplified finding. A growing literature suggests that if individuals go through a series of stressful life events that they are able to control or deal with satisfactorily they may emerge as more competent and resilient individuals than those who have either been overwhelmed by unresolved traumatic experiences or who have encountered little stress in their course of development.

Stress: Theory and Methods

It might seem relatively easy to present an integrated discussion of stress and coping in both children and families. However, it is extremely difficult to provide such a coherent picture. The theory and research on families and children is drawn from different disciplines, which ask different questions and have different preferred research methodologies.

Sociology and Psychiatry

Much of the theorizing and research on stress and coping in families has been done by family sociologists and family systems psychiatrists. A great deal of work on stress in families by sociologists has involved a description of the demographics of family change, including such variables as changing patterns of fertility, marriage, divorce and remarriage, sex roles, and employment. In addition, sociologists have focused on issues of mate selection, marital satisfaction, and the identification of family typologies. This research has been directed almost exclusively toward the adjustment of adults, while until recently the psychological literature was oriented more toward the study of coping in children. The method of choice for such studies has been the survey. Researchers using survey techniques are often preoccupied with obtaining large representative samples but show little concern for establishing the reliability or validity of their measures. Apparently it is assumed in much of this work that people do what they say they do. In contrast, psychologists tend to devote great effort to developing reliable and valid techniques but use small, convenient samples which are often highly selective.

Family systems theory is a second approach that both sociologists and psychiatrists have attempted to use in describing the responses of families to stress. With a few exceptions, such as the innovative work of David Reiss (1981), psychiatrists have confined their efforts to theorizing; consequently, their constructs of family functioning have proven remarkably difficult to operationalize reliably. Constructs such as the double bind, enmeshment, and marital skew and schism are clinically appealing but empirically elusive.

Sociological studies have relied heavily on the use of interviews, questionnaires, and inventories, and only a few have used laboratory analogue family problem-solving tasks. Such analogue tasks have typically been in the tradition of the revealed difference technique (Strodtbeck, 1951), in which subjects who have shared experiences are asked to make individual evaluations of them, and then are asked to reconcile any differences in interpretation. However, family sociologists are much more likely to ask people how they solve their problems than to observe people solving their problems. Family sociologists have emphasized both family vulnerability and the ability to recover from stress. They have focused on the role of the family as a reactor to stress and as a manager of resources within the family that modifies family processes in adapting to stress. Their emphasis has been on internal resources such as cohesion and adaptability that may help the family withstand the stresses it encounters. This focus is found in studies of family coping in response to the absence of fathers because of war or occupational demands, and in the response of families to unemployment, depression, or other disasters. It is only recently in the work of such investigators as McCubbin (McCubbin and others, 1980) that there has been a shift from a focus on the internal organization and functioning of the family to the utilization of social and community resources.

In spite of attempts to characterize the functioning and coping styles of the entire family system, the final result is often a description of the coping of individual family members. In McCubbin's (McCubbin and Lester, 1977) work on prolonged war-induced separation, the change in family structure, the unpredictability of the father's return, and the need for adapting either to the death or return of the father necessitated changes in family relations. However, the most salient factor in the family's coping was the ability of the wives to become self-sufficient, that is, to deal effectively with financial management and gain educational and life experiences that gave them additional skills and prepared them for an independent life.

Another difficulty in attempting to describe the adaptation of the total family system is that the same problems and concerns are not always crucial in coping for adults and children; family members may experience stressful life events in very different ways. The means and ability for solving problems diverge greatly in parents and children. In addition, the needs of children and parents are not always the same — a solution that contributes to the well-being of one may have disastrous outcomes for the other. A good example of this is found in a longitudinal study of divorced mothers, fathers, and their preschool children in the two years following divorce (Hetherington and others, 1982). A group of mothers were identified and labeled as egocentric, self-fulfilling mothers; that is, they recovered most rapidly from any adverse effects of divorce and, by one year after the divorce, reported that their current life was vastly preferable to their married life before. This group of women viewed their current separation as happy, satisfying, and stimulating, and the initial increases in state anxiety, feelings of external control, and low self-esteem, which were found in many women during the first year after divorce, dissapated rapidly. These women returned to school, began to work, became involved with community activities, or pursued social activities and emotional involvements at a frenetic pace. However, they gained their satisfaction at the expense of their children's well-being. The children of these self-fulfilling mothers had the most frequent, intense, and enduring signs of emotional disturbance and behavior problems, both in the home and in the school. This was in part because, in their relentless pursuit of self-gratification and search for a resolution of their own emotional problems, the mothers spent little time with their children and often did not recognize or were unresponsive to their children's needs and distress. The quality of the mothers' relations with their children was hurried, preoccupied, erratic, noncommunicative, and frequently emotionally disengaged. In addition, substitute childcare and supervision were often inadequate.

Wallerstein and Kelly (1980), in their longitudinal study of divorced families with children ranging in ages from one to twenty-two, emphasize that this lack of commonality among the experiences of family members extends back to the marriage and time of separation. Even in marriages in which parents endured years of loneliness, neglect, abuse, and demeaning treatment by their spouse and where divorce seemed the only possible solution to a miserable relationship, children seldom welcomed the dissolution of the marriage. According to Wallerstein and Kelly, few of the children in their study thought that their parents were happily married, yet the overwhelming majority preferred the unhappy marriage to the divorce. "Many of the children, despite the unhappiness of their parents, were relatively happy and considered their situation neither better nor worse than that of other families around them. They would, in fact, have been content to hobble along. The lightning that struck them was the divorce, and they had not been aware of the existence of the storm" (Wallerstein and Kelly, 1980, p. 11).

Psychology

If family systems psychiatrists and family sociologists have focused on the entire family system and neglected individual adaptation, psychologists have erred in the opposite direction. The psychological literature has largely dealt with the adaptation of individuals to stress. In the 1960s, psychologists introduced the concept of the *dyad* and noted the relationship between responses to stress in mothers and children; in the 1970s they included fathers and coined the *triad;* and in the 1980s they are beginning to recognize that the adaptation to stress in families involves a larger cast of characters than the nuclear triad.

Self-report. There has been an interesting shift in the methodology used by psychologists to study families in the past two decades. In the 1960s there was a growing disenchantment with parental reports of behavior. Parental questionnaires, interviews, and ratings of their own or their children's behavior were criticized as providing unreliable, inaccurate, and systematically distorted data. Parents' reports were found to show little relation to their observed behavior.

Direct Observation. The mistrust of self-report methods led to direct observations of parents and children interacting and coping with stress in a variety of situations, ranging from analogue studies and highly structured experimental tasks in the laboratory to free interactions in naturalistic home settings. Of course, such observations are valid only to the extent that representative patterns of interaction have not been disrupted or distorted by the presence of the observer or the demands of the situation. In addition, the usefulness of observations depends entirely on the skill, perceptiveness, and reliability of the observer. A cleverly contrived situation and well-defined behavioral coding categories will be to no avail in the hands of an incompetent observer.

Some of the analogue studies involved such things as the use of higher or low intensity buzzers to simulate highly stressful or less severe punishment. Others involved strangers simulating the role of parents having various attributes—for example, warmth, dominance, or punitiveness. Some of these studies were only irrelevant, others were ludicrous or misleading. Many of these studies were done in an era when rigor was valued over relevance, and the kindest thing that can be said about this work is that it was superbly designed trivia. Baldwin (1967) described developmental psychologists in this period as building a mythology of childhood. Bronfenbrenner (1977) describes the developmental psychology of this time as "the science of the strange behavior of children in strange situations with strange adults for the briefest possible period of time" (p. 513).

Parents and children respond differently when they are interacting with each other than when they are responding to strangers. Parents are less likely to intervene in the noxious antics of a strange child. Children are more responsive to the rewards and reprimands of strangers than of parents in laboratory settings. Married couples when interacting with each other in contrast to strangers are less attentive and positive, more critical and negative, and smile less; wives laugh less at their husbands jokes than at those of a stranger. It cannot be assumed that these simplistic, restricted laboratory interactions of extremely short duration with strangers parallel the family experience in intense, complex, enduring parent-child relations. What is missing in such analogue studies is the past history of the relationship, the beliefs and expectancies associated with it, and the anticipation of a continued relationship.

To encounter these objections, many studies were run with children and parents, rather than strangers, who were observed interacting in stressful or demanding situations in the laboratory. Common situations were chosen in which the mother is preoccupied in attempting to complete a task while children become bored or make bids for attention, where parents must teach children difficult tasks or get them to clean up a disastrously messy playroom, or where parents and children discuss and attempt to resolve areas of family conflict.

Although there are relatively few studies that have observed the same families in multiple settings, the results of those that have suggest that when families are shifted from familiar to unfamiliar settings, from the home to the laboratory, or from semistructured to structured situations, there is a tendency for family members to express less negative emotion, exhibit more socially desirable responses, and assume socially prescribed behavior. Mothers are more directive and less passively attentive in the home than in the laboratory. Similarly, with a shift from the laboratory to the home, there is a change from stereotyped sex-role behavior to an increase in the expression of emotion by fathers and more active participation in decision making by mothers. Even in family problem-solving tasks the responses of family members vary with the specific content of the problem and whether it is a problem actually being experienced by their family or a hypothetical one.

Attempts to minimize such distortions have been made by observing families in familiar situations, permitting a long period of adaptation through frequent observation sessions and the use of unobtrusive measures. Some experiments have monitored homes by television or tape recorders over the entire waking hours of the family. Others have sampled the behavior of families by having their recording instruments activated at random times. Still others have used the kind of mobile monitors carried by physicians. Parents or children are "beeped" at random times and asked to record their behaviors. This permits not only a random sampling of behavior but also of the situations and the social contexts in which these behaviors occur.

What do observers do when they are interested in stress or coping behaviors that occur infrequently and therefore have only a slight chance of being picked up in naturalistic observations? They may wait a long time before seeing a child cheat, steal, have a temper tantrum, or disobey his or her parents. Investigators have resorted to diary records, twenty-four hour behavior checklists such as those used so effectively by Patterson and his colleagues (Patterson, 1982), or techniques such as event recording in which mothers record their children's prosocial behaviors (Radke-Yarrow and others, 1983). In addition, investigators may structure their observational situations in order to elicit stress or coping behaviors. Parents' commands and compliance and noncompliance in children have been effectively studied by letting a young child play in a room with toys with many small pieces or potentially messy equipment—for example, jigsaw puzzles, building blocks, and finger paints—and then asking the mother to have the child clean the room up.

The accelerating interest in observational methodology has led to increasingly molecular observational codes and the study of family process through examining sequences of behavior and behavioral interchanges. Although in the hands of some of the more creative investigators such as Patterson (1982) or Gottman (1979) this molecular sequential coding of behavior has proved fruitful, it has many problems. It is expensive and time-comsuming. Gottman estimates that it takes between 38 and 50 hours of coder time to use stop-frame coding of a single hour of videotaped dyadic interactions. Raters are difficult to train and must be continually retrained. Reliability drift is a problem in live observations where, in contrast to video recorded observations, random and unpredictable reliability checks cannot be made.

In such studies, data reduction also becomes a problem. How do we reduce the plethora of molecular measures into meaningful constructs? Patterson has over eighty measures in his current Parent Adolescent Naturalistic Interaction Code (PANIC) observational scheme. Some investigators use factor analysis, others use functional analysis, and still others use a combination of these methods with face-valid clustering techniques. When clustering or the translation of measures into meaningful constructs is not attempted or is unsuccessful a study often results that is unintelligible or capitalizes on chance relationships in a morass of findings. In some cases important constructs may be translated reliably into observational measures but may not seem to be a true picture of the construct. For example, Gottman (1979) operationalizes power in a family member as the significant increase in the probability of a response in one member changing following a behavior in another, and reciprocity as the successive matching of similar behaviors in interacting dyads. These would seem to be reasonable short-term ways to operationale these constructs; however, families are in long-term relationships that extend both into the past and the future beyond the bounds of the observational sessions. Power in terms of who decides where to go on vacations, or what car to buy, or with which friends to socialize may not be related to short-term shifts in observed conditional probabilities. Similarly, reciprocal behaviors may be delayed. A husband's barbed comments about a wife's slovenly appearance or weight gain at the breakfast table may be reciprocated at dinner with an unappetizing meal or resistance to a forthcoming visit of a mother-in-law.

Multiple Methods. Over late-night brandies or fourth martinis, when investigators are among friends and defenses are down, even some of the most committed observational scientists are starting to express reservations about total reliance on observational methods in limited settings. This has led to a recent increase in the use of multiple method, multiple measure, and multiple setting studies of stress and coping in children and families. Different methods yield different kinds of information, and the information may not be congruent. Cairns (1979) has argued that the techniques that are most effective in describing the outcomes of development may not be effective in analyzing the processes by which social patterns arise and are maintained. It has been suggested that measures such as parental reports should be viewed as a useful source of information about parental attitudes, values, perceptions, and knowledge. They should be used not as a substitute for observational data but as a method that reveals different aspects of family relationships. Radke-Yarrow and others have noted that the skill of the investiagor lies in matching the questions of research with the most appropriate data modes and in obtaining data of the highest fidelity.

Recently, old methods are being used in new ways. In parental interviews, rather than assessment of global attitudes, more highly focused questions about specific behaviors and recent events, such as those used by Rutter, are able to predict children's behavior. Parents' belief systems about such things as the capabilities of their children have been related to child abuse and to parents' and children's behavior when children are attempting to solve problems. Perceptions of behavior may be more important than the behavior itself. Gottman (1979) found that one of the important qualities that distinguished distressed from nondistressed couples was the misinterpretation of behavior in distressed couples. In contrast to nondistressed couples, when a husband or wife in a distressed couple communicated what they believed was a neutral or positive comment the spouse was more likely to perceive it as negative. This awareness of the importance of considering cognitive factors is a strong emergent theme in the study of family interaction. The use of diverse methodologies is yielding a more complex, multifaceted view of children and families coping with stress. Parents and children are seen as feeling, interpreting, evaluating, remembering, anticipating individuals with histories, futures, belief systems, family myths, and values that shape their behaviors and responses to stress.

In addition to the changes in theory and methods of studying families and children by psychologists that have just been discussed, two notable forces have broadened contemporary perspectives on stress and coping. The first is the life-cycle or life-span movement led by such people as Mathilda Riley, Glen Elder, Paul Baltes, and Orville Brim (Baltes and others, 1977; Elder, 1974). The second is the ecological movement led by Urie Bronfenbrenner.

Life-Span Approaches to Stress

Normative and Non-Normative Life Events. The life-cycle approach emphasizes that both individual and families go through a series of developmental changes; there are certain predictable phases in the course of individual and family life cycles and certain specific developmental tasks must be accomplished in these phases. However, the life-span position also emphasizes flexibility of the individual and of the family as they encounter personal and family challenges in each phase. Different coping strategies and patterns of family functioning may be adaptive in different phases of family and personal development. Lewis and others (1974) described this process as follows:

> A competent family self-destructs; children grow up, leave the nest; parents grow old, and, having failing function, die. Adaptation to these stark realities is successful only to the degree that individuation is complete. In such evolved people, a sense of capability does not depend on unchanging relationships. There is an ability to accept the future, to acknowledge and adapt to the great changes brought about by growth and development, aging, and death. A family member can then operate with respect for his own dignity and that of others. He can have joy in encountering a loved one, even though what they encounter brings awareness of the implications of loss and passage of time. When individuation is incomplete, separation is resisted and family pain and functional difficulty increase [p. 203].

Although there are expected events in the life cycle, the trajectory of the path of development can be altered by the way in which individuals respond both to these normative, or predictable events, and to non-normative, unanticipated, or infrequent life events. A normative event might be entrance into school, obtaining a first job, or marriage. Non-normative events include divorce, death of a child, or severe physical illness. Some life-span theorists such as Baltes, Brim, and Kagan have emphasized the discontinuity and lack of predictability in development because of the wide variation in the manner in which people respond to these non-normative events. This concern has led many researchers studying stress and coping to focus on life transitions which serve as nodes or crossroads in development. Short-term longitudinal studies of these transitions have proved particularly useful in identifying what mediates successful and unsuccessful coping with stress. However, there is no single route but rather multiple pathways to both adaptive and maladaptive outcomes in response to stress.

Historical Cohort Effects. Life-span theorists also emphasize the importance of historical or secular changes in the study of stress and coping. The experience of stress and one's response to it may vary widely with different historical cohorts. For example, the annual rate of divorce has increased temporarily after every major war in which the United States was involved, including the Civil War, World War I, and World War II (Cherlin, 1978). The problems of hurried, impulsive marriages, separation and reunion, and the experience of war impose multiple stresses on human relationships. In addition, the Depression lowered the divorce rate in the 1930s and there is evidence that there has been a slowing in the divorce rate with the current recession of the early 1980s. Does that mean that financial stress contributes to marital happiness? It is more likely that, with housing expensive and jobs unavailable, many couples are unable to afford to divorce and have to delay divorcing until they can afford it. Elder's work on the Great Depression (Elder, 1974) and that of Komarovsky (1940) in her well-known study of the unemployed man and his family suggest that secular changes, such as economic depressions and the stresses accompanying them, may affect the family with major changes in family functioning, role reversals, and some unanticipated long-term outcomes. Komarovsky describes family dynamics, where paternal unemployment and dire economic exigencies led to wives and teen-aged children, especially teenaged sons, being forced to obtain jobs if they could. A husband who became unemployed lost more than his job—he lost his status, power, and respect in the household. The employed teenaged son often assumed the privileges and roles held by the father when he was the family breadwinner.

An employed seventeen-year-old son, Henry Brady, described his situation as follows: "I'm my own boss now. Nobody can tell me what to do or how to spend my money. Working makes you feel independent. I remind them who makes the money. They don't say much. They just take it, that's all. I'm not the one on relief. I can't help feeling that way" (Komarovsky, 1940, p. 100). Henry added that seeing his father so discouraged and without ambition made him lose respect for him. "He is not the same father, that's all. You can't help not looking up to him like we used to" (p. 101). Komarovsky poignantly describes a dinner table scene: Henry walks in, and there are no available chairs. Mr. Brady rises and meekly yields his place to his son. Henry, with no thanks or regard for his father's feelings, takes his place at the table as if it is his prerogative.

Elder's (1974) work on the Great Depression substantiates this loss of status of fathers and the lack of closeness and respect between adolescent children and their unemployed fathers. In addition, changes in role relationships led to some long-term outcomes for the children. Elder describes the experiences of the adolescent boys and girls from severely economically deprived families as "the downward extension of adult-like experience" (1974, p. 80). Girls participated more in household tasks and childcare; boys were employed, independent, and actively involved with peers and extrafamilial activities. These adolescents grew up to value family life, and they married and had children earlier than did their nondeprived peers or cohorts who were adolescents before or after the Depression. Elder suggests that these adolescents came to view a cohesive family as a desirable resource because a stable family relationship had been unavailable during times of economic hardship. Easterlin (1968) offers an alternative explanation for the early marriages of this cohort. He suggests that a person's standard of living is determined by the economic conditions experienced in growing up, especially in adolescence. Thus, adolescents growing up during the Depression were satisfied with a modest level of material goods. When they had a job with a modest income they felt that they could maintain what they viewed as a reasonable standard of living for themselves, a wife, and children. In contrast, adolescents who grew up in the affluent 1950s and 1960s delayed marriage and childbirth because of their more aggrandized perspective of an acceptable standard of living. Here the importance of cognitive factors—that is, the interpretation of events—in the outcomes of stress and coping is apparent.

Although life-cycle theorists have alerted us to the importance of examining individual and family developmental changes, normative and nonnormative life events, and secular change in studying stress and coping, their perspective has not had a major impact on research in this area, with the exception of the study of life transitions. The interface between personal individuation and the tasks of the family life cycle are rarely examined. The cohort designs proposed by Schaie, Baltes, and Nesselroade (Schaie and others, 1974; Nesselroade and Baltes, 1979) are impressive and reasonable but cumbersome to execute, often requiring an unreasonable number of subjects. Even naturalistic studies of secular change have been criticized by Bronfenfrenner (1977) as "being limited to variations of cultural or social change that presently exist or that have occurred in the past. Future possibilities remain uncharted except by hazardous exploitation" (Bronfenfrenner, 1977, p. 528).

The Ecological Approach to Stress

A final perspective that recently has had great impact on research in stress and coping is that of the developmental ecologists. Bronfenbrenner (1977) proposes that to understand the impact of stress and variations in coping one has to examine the progressive accommodations children and families make to the environments in which they live. The environment includes not only the immediate setting, which contains the developing child and family, but also the larger social contexts, both formal and informal, in which the child or family is embedded. This position has stimulated a great deal of exciting research. Variations in stresses encountered by family members and in the coping mechanisms used in a variety of settings have been examined. The moderating effects of social networks and social systems external to the family on outcomes of stress are being studied (Gore, 1978). However, one of the difficulties encountered in such work is the lack of a conceptual framework for describing and identifying the salient dimensions of environments and social systems.

In summary, significant progress is being made in the conceptual framework and the methodology being used to study stress and coping in children and families. More meaningful questions are being asked; more appropriate, varied, and sophisticated methodologies are being used; and more informative systems of data analysis are being applied. Investigators are becoming less defensive about their methods and more aware of the complexity of the problems that remain to be solved in the study of stress and coping.

Research on Stress and Coping

Some of the research findings on the responses of children and families to stress will now be presented to raise the important conceptual issues in this area. The adaptation to stress is based on an interaction between past and present life hardships and stressful life experiences, the protagonist's interpretation of the situation, and the available personal, familial, and extrafamilial resources that can be used to deal with the stressful events.

Stress and Coping as Transition Experiences

Both stress and coping need to be viewed as events or processes that extend over time. They involve a sequence of experiences associated with transitions in the lives of children and parents. The point at which researchers tap into this sequence will affect their view of the responses of parents and children to stress. Certain consequences of stress emerge rapidly, some increase over time and then abate, and still others show a delayed emergence. It is important to distinguish between the consequences of stress that are related to temporary emotional distress and those that involve a delay or more enduring deviation in the life cycle or course of development.

Different factors may shape the adaptation of individuals to stress at different points in time. The example of divorce as a crisis model may be most appropriate in conceptualizing the short-term effects of divorce on children. In the period during and immediately following divorce the child may be responding to changes in his or her life situations—to loss of a parent, to the marital discord and family disorganization that usually precede and accompany separation, to alterations in the parent–child relationship that may be associated with temporary distress and emotional neediness of family members, and to other real or fantasied threats to the well-being of the child that are elicited by the uncertainty of the situation. In this period, stresses associated with conflict, loss, change, and uncertainty may be the critical factors.

The research evidence suggests that most children can cope and adapt to the short-term crisis of divorce within a few years; however, if the crisis is compounded by multiple stresses and continued adversity, developmental disruptions may occur. The longer-term adjustment of the child is related to more sustained or concurrent conditions associated with growing up in a one-parent household. These involve factors directly related to the parent–child relationship, such as changes in the quality of parent–child interactions; the increased importance of the custodial parent; the lack of availability of the noncustodial parent; and the presence of fewer significant adults in the household to participate in decision making, to serve as models, disciplinarians, or sources of nurturance, or to assume responsibility for childcare and household tasks. Other factors affecting the long-term outcome of divorce for children may not be directly mediated by parent–child relations. They may involve changing support systems, altered economic resources, and changed relationships in extrafamilial settings such as the neighborhood, peer group, and school. It seems reasonable to assume that as the salient factors shift in different phases following a stressful life event some discontinuities in the coping and adjustment of individuals in response to stress will occur.

Personal Perception and Expectations in Stress

Many investigators have emphasized the key role that a person's perception of a life event plays in responding to stress. For example, pregnancy may be perceived as a highly desirable event for a woman who has been taking fertility pills, but not for an unmarried teenager or for a fifty-year-old woman who is just beginning to enjoy the peace and freedom of the empty nest.

Even different members of the same family may perceive the same life event in very disparate ways. This is particularly evident during marital dissolution. Since divorce usually involves intense emotion, acrimony, and change, it is not surprising that the perception of divorce and expectations about life experiences associated with marital dissolution vary among members of the same family. Bernard (1972) has observed that if investigators talk of "his and her" marriages, they should also talk of "his and her" divorces. When husbands and wives describe their marriage or divorce, it is often difficult to recognize that the same relationship is involved (Bernard, 1972; Chiriboga and Cutler, 1978; Hetherington and others, 1982; Levinger, 1966; Scanzoni, 1968; Weiss, 1975). In giving reasons for marital dissolution, women most often complain of lack of affection and communication from their husbands or infidelity; men talk of problems of sexual incompatibility and relationships with in-laws. Weiss (1975) calls these descriptions of the marital breakdown "accounts." Variations in accounts are associated with social class, sex, race, age, and personality. Accounts are modified and elaborated over time. It has been proposed that the altered perceptions and social meanings attached to the divorce process may help the family make the experience seem more rational and suggest ways to overcome the stressful situation (Gerhardt, 1979; Venters, 1979). However, it seems likely that if perceptions among family members are too divergent so far removed from reality, family problem solving will be hindered rather than facilitated (Gottman, 1979). There has been no study directed at elucidating psychological processes such as dissonance reduction and attribution that may mediate variations in accounts.

Just as there are variations in the perception of stress, there are great differences in expectations about what life will be like following stressful events. In divorce, expectations about such things as anticipated poverty, loneliness, independence, or opportunities for self-actualization may be as important as the actual changes that occur in adjusting to family stress and divorce (Boss, 1977; Howard, 1974; McCubbin and Patterson, 1981). Sarason (1980) has suggested that an individual's reaction to stress involves two kinds of appraisals: an appraisal of the situation and an appraisal of the individual's ability to deal successfully with it. The most adaptive response to stress is a problem-solving orientation that focuses on the task rather than on emotional reactions. There is some evidence that, following divorce, women who focus on improving their earning capacity through skills training or education, confront the problems of raising children alone, and actively seek out social contacts recover from divorce more rapidly than those who focus on hostility or longing for the departed spouse and feelings of self-castigation, self-pity, or guilt.

Personal Resources and Characteristics

The response to stress also will be modified by the characteristics of the child and family and the resources available in the family for the management of stress. These include personal resources such as financial, educational, health, and psychological resources, and individual characteristics such as personality, temperament, skills, intelligence, age, and sex (George, 1980). In addition, family resources such as cohesion, adaptability, communication and problem-solving skills (Burr, 1973; Olson and others, 1979; McCubbin and others, 1980) and social supports (Hetherington and others, 1982; Hess and Camara, 1979; Kitson and Raschke, 1981) such as neighbor, kin, and friendship networks, and self-help groups are important in coping with stressful life events.

Temperament and Personality. Temperamentally difficult children have been found to be less adaptable to change and more vulnerable to adversity than are temperamentally easy children. Rutter (1979a, 1979b) has noted that the increased risk of the temperamentally difficult child is in part attributable to transactions with the parents. The difficult child is more likely to be both the elicitor and the target of aversive responses by the parent; while in times of family disharmony or stress the temperamentally easy child is not only less likely to be the recipient of criticism and displaced anger and anxiety, but also is more able to cope with it when it hits.

Independence and nontraditional sex roles are related to coping in women (Brown and others, 1977; Brown and Manela, 1978; Granvold and others, 1979; Hetherington and others, 1982). High self-esteem, low anxiety, feelings of internal control, open mindedness, and tolerance for change are associated with low distress and ease of adjustment to stress for both men and women (Chiriboga and Cutler, 1978; Hetherington and others, 1982; Pais, 1978; Spanier and Casto, 1979; Wallerstein and Kelly, 1980; Weiss, 1975). In addition, family factors such as low conflict, mutual support between spouses or between parents and children, and family cohesiveness are related to adaptability.

Developmental Status. Throughout the life span, events are experienced as most stressful by individuals if they occur at times that are inappropriate for his or her stage in the life cycle (Hultsch and Plemons, 1979). The birth of a baby, departure or return of offspring, death of a spouse, or retirement have most impact on adults if they occur out of phase.

The resources and adaptive abilities of children and families vary with their developmental or life course status. The limited social and cognitive competencies of the young child, the child's dependence on parents, and his or her more exclusive restriction to the home situation will be associated with different stresses, resources, and responses than those of the more mature, skillful, and independent older child. Young children are less able to understand a stressful event such as death or divorce, the behavior and feelings of others, their contribution to and influence on the situation, or to evaluate possible outcomes. With age, children become increasingly able to appraise the complex array of factors associated with the stressful event, to understand the motives and behavior of other people involved in the situation, and to respond in a constructive, task-oriented fashion (Wallerstein and Kelly, 1980). Although positive relations with parents continue to play an important role in the adjustment of adolescents, older children do have many more resources available outside of the home. Older children can find sources of support and gratification in the peer group, school, neighborhood, and work place that can help to counter the negative effects of an adverse home situation (Hetherington, 1981; Hetherington and others, 1982).

The importance of the age of the child varies with the stressful event being experienced. Studies of both hospitalization of children and those in daycare suggest that the greatest stress is experienced after the period of specific attachment (about six to ten months in age), before three or four, when children are cognitively mature enough to recognize that separation does not mean rejection or permanent loss. In contrast, although young children seem to experience less intense immediate responses to death of a parent than do older children, there is some suggestion that more severe delayed long-term effects may occur for the younger children.

A different pattern emerges for divorce. Although it has been proposed that the effects of divorce will be more adverse for younger children, research findings are not consistent in supporting this position. It is more accurate to say that coping styles and the evolution of patterns of adjustment over time differ for children of various ages, rather than that adjustment is easier or more difficult for some age groups than others. Wallerstein and Kelly (1980) report that, although preschool children are the most emotionally disturbed at eighteen months after separation, the younger children and adolescents appear to be coping better than latency-aged children four years after separation.

Since Wallerstein and Kelly are the only investigators who have done a longitudinal study of the adjustment of children of different ages to divorce, their findings will be drawn upon for much of the following discussion. Pervasive sadness, loneliness, grieving for the lost parent, anger, anxiety, and feelings of rejection are common emotions experienced by children of all ages around the time of separation (Wallerstein and Kelly, 1980). However, the intensity and duration of these feelings vary for children of different ages. The egocentrism and restricted cognitive and social skills of the young child lead him or her to be more self-blaming in interpreting the cause of divorce and to distort grossly perceptions of the parents' emotions, needs, and behavior and of the prospects of reconciliation or total abandonment (Tessman, 1978; Wallerstein and Kelly, 1980).

Great ambivalence in interpersonal relations appears in these young children; they exhibit clinging and excessive dependency combined with hostile, angry responses and sometimes indiscriminate affectional overtures toward adults, especially adult males. In the study by Hetherington and others (1982), during the crisis period of divorce, preschool boys from the mother-headed families made overtures toward male teachers almost twice as often as did boys in the nondivorced families. This occurred more frequently with boys who had had a close predivorce relationship with their fathers and now had little contact with them. Wallerstein and Kelly (1980) also report that young boys who had highly involved, positive relationships with their fathers showed intense initial anguish in response to separation.

Although elementary school-aged children are distressed and depressed at separation, they are more able to be sympathetic and concerned in response to the difficulties and traumas being experienced by their parents. Their lessening egocentrism is also accompanied by concern about what others think of them, their parents, and their situation. In older latency-aged children this sometimes involves putting up a front and concealing feelings from family and friends. Anger is often used as a defense against depression and concerns about loss of love. Although anger tends to diminish in most children following divorce, it is more often sustained in the form of explosive outbursts and temper tantrums in nine- and ten-year-old boys. If the aggression is viewed as a defense against depression, it is a notably unsuccessful one, since the most sustained depression is likely to be found in latency-aged children and those just entering adolescence.

Wallerstein and Kelly note that great variability in behavior in the school situation is found in latency-aged children following separation. For some children, severe academic disruptions occur; however, for others who had been freed from a particularly conflicted family situation or an aversive relationship with a father, academic striving and achievement may soar after restabilization of the family unit occurs. Wallerstein and Kelly rely on teachers' reports for this information and not on standardized tests or grades.

Although most adolescents experience considerable initial pain and anger when their parents divorce, when the immediate trauma of divorce is over they are more able to assign accurately responsibility for the divorce, resolve loyalty conflicts, and assess and cope with economic and other practical exigencies (Wallerstein and Kelly, 1980). They try to test and evaluate changing perceptions of themselves and their parents, often using the consensual validation of people outside of the family such as peers and teachers. Adolescents are more able than younger children to consider realistically the complex interactive network of factors that contributed to the divorce and the broad array of possible outcomes in their new life situation. In addition, adolescents, more than younger children, do have the option to disengage and seek gratification elsewhere if the home situation is particularly painful (Weiss, 1975). However, it should be noted that this adolescent disengagement often involves a premature destructive detachment from the family and avoidance of contact with the parents or an escape from the present by becoming extremely involved in future plans and goals.

Sex. It has been proposed that males are more vulnerable than females to stress. Even in the primate studies of early isolation, male monkeys were more severely and permanently disrupted by isolation. Human males seem to be more adversely affected by daycare, birth of a sibling, and to some extent by hospitalization. Boys are more severely affected by family conflict in both one- and two-parent households than are girls. Both conflict between spouses or ex-spouses and between parents and children is associated with the development of behavior disorders in children (Emery, 1982; Emery and O'Leary, 1982; Hess and Camara, 1979; Hetherington and others, 1982; McDermott, 1968, 1970; Wallerstein and Kelly, 1980; Westman and others, 1970; Rutter, 1979a, 1979b, 1983). Interparental conflict to which the child has not been directly exposed does not appear to be associated with psychopathology in children (Hetherington and others, 1982; Rutter, 1979b). The relationship between family conflict and behavior disorders is closer and more consistently found for boys than girls (Cadoret and Cain, 1980; Block and others, 1981;

Emery and O'Leary, 1982; Hess and Camara, 1979; Hetherington and others, 1982; Porter and O'Leary, 1980; Rutter, 1971; Wolkind and Rutter, 1973). When family conflict occurs, boys are more often exposed to the battles and disagreements and get less support than do girls (Hetherington and others, 1982). In addition, boys are more prone to respond to stressful situations with less control; girls are overcontrolled (Emery, 1982). Undercontrol, particularly when it takes the combination of aggressiveness, noncompliance, and demandingness found in stressed boys, may be particularly likely to turn off compassionate responses in others. There also is a suggestion that males interpret family disagreements less favorably than do females (Epstein and others, 1979).

Family Resources and Support Systems

The effects of life events are moderated by both intra- and extrafamilial support systems. However, when families are going through a major stressful event, there may be major changes in parent–child relations that exacerbate the effects of stress. When families are undergoing severe stress the emotional disturbance experienced by each family member may escalate that of the others. Angry, preoccupied, worried, or depressed parents and anxious, demanding children may find it difficult to be responsive and mutually supportive. Family cohesiveness seems to be particularly important in times of stress. Even in families that are lacking in cohesiveness, an exceptionally good relationship with one parent may buffer the adverse effects of stressful life events or a relationship with an antisocial, rejecting, or abusive parent. Such a negative relationship seems to be a problem in one-parent households. If there is a poor relationship between a custodial parent and child the noncustodial parent, who is not there to mediate in day-to-day altercations, is not an effective buffer (Hetherington and others, 1982).

Support systems, such as extended kin groups, friendships, church and neighborhood groups, and self-help groups, have been found to have positive effects in reducing the negative effects of stress. Social isolation is related to disruptions in family functioning and an inability to deal with stress in both one- and two-parent households. Married couples rely less on external supports than do divorced, single, or widowed adults. Support from friends and family have been found to facilitate the parenting role and to be associated with life satisfaction, personal growth, and a sense of security in both men and women.

Although recently there has been concern about generational fragmentation in families, most older persons maintain satisfying supportive and close relations with their adult children. The support exchanged varied for different social classes. Lower-class families tend to give support in the form of services, while middle-class families give economic or material support.

The relationship with kin following divorce is a complex one. The interaction between the divorced adult and his or her parents continues and contacts may increase following divorce, but contact with relatives and in-laws decreases (Anspach, 1976; Duffy, 1981; Spicer and Hampe, 1975). The child's relations with the kin of the noncustodial parent is mediated through contact with the noncustodial parent, which may be infrequent. Relatives, especially grandparents, frequently provide financial and emotional support and assistance in childcare (Furstenberg, 1979; Hetherington and others, 1982; Shanas, 1979); however, the extent of this support may be moderated by the relatives' approval of the decision to divorce (Kitson and others, 1980). The increased contact with the mother's own kin, particularly the children's grandparents, has been shown to have positive effects on lone mothers and children (Kellam and others, 1977; 1982). The mental health of children in a home with a mother and grandmother is considerably better than that in a home with a mother alone. However, it is often difficult for a divorced or unmarried woman to live with her own mother. The mother's own needs for independence are often threatened and conflicts about childrearing may arise. Most divorced mothers prefer to set up an independent household when they have financial resources and adequate childcare facilities available. Friends and neighbors also often provide some form of aid to single-parent families, such as help in emergencies, childcare, transportation, shopping, and money (Bernard, 1972; Colletta, 1979; Hetherington and others, 1982).

In addition to divorce, social supports have been found to play a prominent role when individuals and families confront job problems and unemployment (Gore, 1978), physical and emotional illness, complications of childbirth, death, and natural disasters (Bloom, 1983).

Extrafamilial Support Systems

Schools and Peers. Most of the work on support systems has been done on adults, and that which has dealt with support systems for children has focused mainly on the family and kin networks. Although we know that "aloneness" is a problem for adults, for children the role of extrafamilial supports, peers, schools, neighborhoods, the church, and social groups such as clubs or athletic groups has not been examined.

For preschool children, family relations are important in the adjustment to stress. Disruptions in family functioning are associated with maladaptive behaviors both in the home and in other social situations (Hess and Camara, 1979; Hetherington and others, 1982; Hetherington, 1981; Wallerstein and Kelly, 1980). Older children are able to use peers and schools as sources of information, satisfaction, and support (Hetherington and others, 1982; Wallerstein and Kelly, 1980). The validation of self-worth, competence, and personal control is an important function served by peers and the school. Constructive relationships with teachers and peers and a positive school and neighborhood environment can somewhat attenuate the effects of stressful events and nonsupportive family relations (Hess and Camara, 1979; Hetherington and others, 1982; Rutter, 1978; Rutter and others, 1979; Wallerstein and Kelly, 1980).

Rutter (Rutter and others, 1979) has found that certain schools seem to reduce markedly absenteeism and antisocial behavior in children from high-risk neighborhoods and families. The study by Hetherington and others (1982) found that in the crisis period following their parents' divorce children adjusted best in a school setting in which there was a relatively structured and predictable environment and in which routines and activities followed regular schedules. In addition, the attentiveness, warmth, and supportiveness of the teacher and the assignment of responsibility to the child were associated with positive adjustment. These are similar to the attributes of the protective schools in the study by Rutter and others (1979). In the study by Hetherington and others (1982) these relationships between adjustment and attributes of the school were higher for the children of divorced than nondivorced parents and more marked for children in conflict-ridden, intact families than in low-conflict non-divorced families. The salutary school characteristics are similar to the characteristics of parental discipline—authoritative control, consistency, maturity demands, and nurturance—that are associated with a low incidence of behavior disorders in the home following stress. A structured, predictable environment seems particularly important to young children going through a stressful transition. It is less important to nonstressed children and may well be less important to older children who are better able to structure their own environment.

Resilience in Children and Families

This presentation concludes with a brief discussion of individuals who have been called "invulnerable" or "resilient"; who when confronted with stress cope more rapidly and effectively with it than others. They seem to endure extremely stressful lives and emerge as competent, happy, creative individuals. Some of the protective factors we have discussed seem to play a part in their development; however, Rachman (1979) advanced an intriguing notion of a factor that he calls "required helpfulness" that may play a major role in this apparent resilience. Rachman writes:

The concept was introduced in recognition of the fact that people who are required to carry out dangerous/difficult tasks that are socially desirable often manage to do so effectively and without strain... Required helpfulness refers to dangerous/difficult acts that are performed in response to social requirements—in order to reduce or prevent other people from experiencing serious discomfort. Under the incentive of high social demands, helpers often act more effectively and more persistently than at other times. The execution of successful acts of required helpfulness may lead to enduring changes in the helper himself. It is probable that in addition to the formally provided training for helping. . .execution of the required tasks, followed by the appropriate feedback, will lead to the growth of new coping skills (1979, p 4).

Garmezy (1983) describes required helpfulness as "therapy through helping others, and its consequences include increased competence in the helper, markedly heightened morale, a marked increment in motivation and persistence, a heightened probability of successful accomplishment of one's tasks, a greater toleration of discomfort evoked by its performance, and the acquisition of new skills that lifts the level of performance past its previous asymptote" (p. 128).

Conclusion

The study of stress and coping has advanced to the point where both theoretical models and research methodology are increasingly sophisticated; they capitalize on the diverse strengths and contributions of a variety of disciplines. Scientists working on stress and coping are not only able to explain and predict some of the responses to stress but are beginning to be able to engineer ways to avert stressful events or to improve the individual's adjustment to them. Preventive intervention programs are being initiated both to reduce the probability that stressful life events will occur for children and families and to increase the ability of children and parents to cope with stress (Bloom, 1983). In addition, there has been a shift from examining only why people are unable to adapt to hardship to studying how people not only adjust to but are personally enhanced by coping with stress. These advances and perspectives seem likely to lead to practices and policies that can promote the healthy development of children and strengthen family life.

References

Anspach, D. F. "Kinship and Divorce." *Journal of Marriage and the Family,* 1976, *38,* 343–350.

Baldwin, A. L. *Theories of Child Development.* (1st ed.) New York: Wiley, 1967.

Baltes, P. R., Reese, H. W., and Nesselroade, J. R. *Life-Span Developmental Psychology: Introduction to Research Methods.* Monterey, Calif.: Brookes/Cole, 1977.

Bernard, J. *The Future of Marriage.* New York: Bantam, 1972.

Block, J. H., Block, J., and Morrison, A. "Parental Agreement-Disagreement on Childrearing Orientations and Gender-Related Personality Correlates in Children." *Child Development,* 1981, *52,* 965–974.

Bloom, B. L. *Stressful Life Event Theory and Research: Implications for Primary Prevention.* Paper prepared for the National Institute of Mental Health, 1983.

Boss, P. "A Clarification of the Concept of Psychological Father Presence in Families Experiencing Ambiguity of Boundary." *Journal of Marriage and the Family,* 1977, *39,* 141–151.

Bronfenbrenner, U. "Toward an Experimental Ecology of Human Development." *American Psychologist,* 1977, *32,* 513–531.

Brown, P., and Manela, R. "Changing Family Roles: Women and Divorce." *Journal of Divorce,* 1978, *4,* 315–328.

Brown, P., Perry, L., and Harburg, E. "Sex-role Attitudes and Psychological Outcomes for Black and White Women Experiencing Marital Dissolution." *Journal of Marriage and the Family,* 1977, *39,* 549–561.

Burr, W. F. *Theory Construction and the Sociology of the Family.* New York: Wiley, 1973.

Cadoret, R., and Cain, C. "Sex Differences in Predictors of Antisocial Behavior in Adoptees." *Archives of General Psychiatry,* 1980, *37,* 1171–1175.

Cairns, R. "Toward Guidelines for Interactional Research." In R. Cairns (Ed.), *The Analysis of Social Interactions: Methods, Issues, and Illustrations.* Hillsdale, N.J.: Erlbaum, 1979.

Cherlin, A. "Remarriage as an Incomplete Institution." *American Journal of Sociology,* 1978, *84,* 634–650.

Chiriboga, D. A., and Cutler, L. "Stress Responses Among Divorcing Men and Women." *Journal of Divorce,* 1978, *1,* 95–105.

Chiriboga, D. A., Roberts, J., and Stein, J. A. "Psychological Well-Being During Marital Separation." *Journal of Divorce,* 1978, *2,* 21–36.

Colletta, M. D. "Support Systems After Divorce: Incidence and Impact." *Journal of Marriage and the Family,* 1979, *41,* 837–846.

Duffy, M. "Divorce and the Dynamics of the Family Kinship System." *Journal of Divorce,* 1981, *5,* 3–18.

Dunn, J., and Kendrick, C. "The Arrival of a Sibling: Changes in Patterns of Interaction Between Mother and First-Born Child." *Journal of Child Psychology and Psychiatry,* 1980, *21,* 119–132.

Easterlin, R. A. *Population, Labor Force, and Long Swings in Economic Growth.* New York: Columbia University Press, 1968.

Elder, G. H., Jr. *Children of the Great Depression.* Chicago: University of Chicago Press, 1974.

Emery, R. E. "Marital Turmoil: Interpersonal Conflict and the Children of Discord and Divorce." *Psychological Bulletin,* 1982, *92,* 310–330.

Emery, R. E., and O'Leary, K. D. "Children's Perceptions of Marital Discord and Behavior Problems of Boys and Girls." *Journal of Abnormal Child Psychology,* 1982, *10,* 11–24.

Epstein, N., Finnegan, D., and Gythell, D. "Irrational Beliefs and Perceptions of Marital Conflict." *Journal of Consulting and Clinical Psychology,* 1979, *67,* 608–609.

Furstenberg, F. F., Jr. *Unplanned Parenthood: The Social Consequences of Teenage Childrearing.* New York: Free Press, 1976.

Furstenberg, F. F., Jr. *Remarriage and Intergenerational Relations.* Paper presented at a workshop on stability and change, March 1979, Annapolis, Md.

Garmezy, N. *Stress-Resistant Children: The Search for Protective Factors.* Paper presented at the 10th International Congress of the International Association for Child and Adolescent Psychiatry and Allied Professions, July 1982, Dublin, Ireland.

Garmezy, N. "Stressors in Childhood." In N. Garmezy and M. Rutter (Eds.), *Stress Coping, and Development in Children.* New York: McGraw-Hill, 1983.

George, L. *Role Transitions in Later Life.* Belmont, Calif.: Brooks/Cole, 1980.

Gerhardt, V. "Coping and Social Action: Theoretical Reconstruction of the Life Event Approach." *Sociology of Health and Illness,* 1979, *1,* 195–225.

Gore, S. "The Effect of Social Support in Moderating the Health Consequences of Unemployment." *Journal of Health and Social Behavior,* 1978, *2,* 157–165.

Gottman, J. M. *Marital Interaction: Experimental Investigations.* New York: Academic Press, 1979.

Granvold, D. K., Pedler, L. M., and Schellie, S. G. "A Study of Sex-Role Expectancy and Female Post-Divorce Adjustment." *Journal of Divorce*, 1979, *2*, 383–393.

Hess, R. D., and Camara, K. A. "Post-Divorce Family Relationships as Mediating Factors in the Consequences of Divorce for Children." *Journal of Social Issues*, 1979, *35*, 79–96.

Hetherington, E. M. "Children and Divorce." In R. Henderson (Ed.), *Parent-Child Interaction: Theory, Research, and Prospect*. New York: Academic Press, 1981.

Hetherington, E. M., Cox, M., and Cox, R. "Effects of Divorce on Parents and Children." In M. Lamb (Ed.), *Nontraditional Families*. Hillsdale, N.J.: Erlbaum, 1982.

Howard, A. *Ain't No Big Thing: Coping Strategies in a Hawaiian-American Community*. Honolulu: University of Hawaii Press, 1974.

Hultsch, D. F., and Plemons, J. K. *Life-Span Development and Behavior*. Vol. 2. New York: Academic Press, 1979.

Kellam, S. G., Ensminger, M. A., and Turner, J. T. "Family Structure and the Mental Health of Children." *Archives of General Psychiatry*, 1977, *34*, 1012–1022.

Kellam, S. G., Adams, R. G., Brown, C. H., and Ensminger, M. A. "The Longer-Term Evolution of the Family Structure of Teenage and Older Mothers." *Journal of Marriage and the Family*, 1982, *4*, 539–554.

Kitson, G. C., Moir, R. N., and Mason, P. R. *Family Social Support in Crises: The Special Case of Divorce*. Unpublished manuscript, Case Western Reserve University, Cleveland, Ohio, 1980.

Kitson, G. C., and Raschke, H. J. "Divorce Research: What We Know; What We Need to Know." *Journal of Divorce*, 1981, *4*, 1–37.

Komarovsky, M. *The Unemployed Man and His Family*. New York: Dryden Press, 1940.

Levinger, G. "Sources of Marital Dissatisfaction Among Applicants for Divorce." *American Journal of Orthopsychiatry*, 1966, *36*, 803–807.

Lewis, J. M., Beavers, W. R., Gossett, J. T., and Phillips, V. A. *No Single Thread: Psychological Health in Family Systems*. New York: Brunner-Mazel, 1974.

McCubbin, H. I., Joy, C. B., Cauble, E. A., Comeau, J. K., Patterson, J. M., and Needle, R. H. "Family Stress and Coping: A Decade Review." *Journal of Marriage and the Family*, 1980, *42*, 855–871.

McCubbin, H., and Lester, G. *Family Adaptability: Coping Behaviors in the Management of the Dual Stressors of Family Separation and Reunion*. Paper presented at the Military Family Research Conference, San Diego, September 1977.

McCubbin, H. I. and Patterson, J. M. *Family Stress and Adaptation to Crises: A Double ABCX Model of Family Behavior*. Paper presented at the annual meeting of the National Council on Family Relations, Milwaukee, October 1981.

McDermott, J. F. "Parental Divorce in Early Childhood." *American Journal of Psychiatry*, 1968, *124*, 1424–1432.

McDermott, J. F. "Divorce and Its Psychiatric Sequelae in Children." *Archives of General Psychiatry*, 1970, *32*, 421–427.

Nesselroade, J. R., and Baltes, P. B. *Longitudinal Research in the Study of Behavioral Development*. New York: Academic Press, 1979.

Olson, D. H., Sprenkle, D. H., and Russell, C. S. "Circumplex Model of Marital and Family Systems: Cohesion and Adaptability Dimensions, Family Types, and Clinical Applications." *Family Process*, 1979, *18*, 3–28.

Pais, J. S. *Social-Psychological Predictions of Adjustment for Divorced Mothers*. Unpublished doctoral dissertation, University of Tennessee, Knoxville, 1978.

Patterson, G. R. *Coercive Family Process*. Eugene, Ore.: Castalia, 1982.

Paykel, E. S. "Life Stress and Psychiatric Disorder: Applications of the Clinical Approach." In B. S. Dohrenwend and B. P. Dohrenwend (Eds.), *Stressful Life Events: Their Nature and Effects*. New York: Wiley, 1974.

32

Porter, B., and O'Leary, K. D. "Types of Marital Discord and Child Behavior Problems." *Journal of Abnormal Child Psychology*, 1980, *8*, 287–295.

Rachman, S. J. "The Concept of Required Helpfulness." *Behavior Research and Therapy*, 1979, *17*, 1–6.

Radke-Yarrow, M., Zahn-Waxler, C., and Chapman, M. "Children's Prosocial Disposition and Behavior." In E. M. Hetherington (Ed.), *Handbook of Child Psychology: Socialization, Personality, and Social Development.* Vol. 4. New York: Wiley, 1983.

Reiss, D. *The Family's Construction of Reality.* Cambridge, Mass.: Harvard University Press, 1981.

Rutter, M. "Parent-Child Separation: Psychological Effects on the Children." *Journal of Child Psychology and Psychiatry and Allied Disciplines,* 1971, *12*, 233–260.

Rutter, M. "Family, Area, and School Influence in the Genesis of Conduct Disorders." In L. A. Hersov and D. Shaffer (Eds.), *Aggression and Anti-Social Behavior in Childhood and Adolescence.* New York: Pergamon Press, 1978.

Rutter, M. "Protective Factors in Children's Responses to Stress and Disadvantage." In M. W. Kent and J. E. Rolf (Eds.), *Primary Prevention of Psychopathology.* Vol. 3. Hanover, N.J.: University Press of New England, 1979a.

Rutter, M. "Maternal Deprivation, 1972–1978: New Findings, New Concepts, New Approaches." *Child Development,* 1979b, *50,* 283–305.

Rutter, M. "Developmental Psychopathology." In E. M. Hetherington (Ed.), *Handbook of Child Psychology: Socialization, Personality, and Social Development.* Vol. 4. New York: Wiley, 1983.

Rutter, M., Maughan, B., Mortimore, P., Ouston, J., and Smith, A. *Fifteen Thousand Hours: Secondary Schools and Their Effects on Children.* Cambridge, Mass.: Harvard University Press, 1979.

Sarason, I. G. "Life Stress, Self-Preoccupation, and Social Support." In L. G. Sarason and C. D. Spielberger (Eds.), *Stress and Anxiety.* Vol. 7. Washington, D.C.: Halsted, 1980.

Scanzoni, J. "A Social System Analysis of Dissolved and Existing Marriages." *Journal of Marriage and the Family,* 1968, *30,* 452–461.

Schaie, K., Labouvie, G. V., and Buech, B. U. "Generational and Cohort-Specific Difference in Adult Cognitive Functioning: A Fourteen-Year Cross-Sequential Study." *Developmental Psychology,* 1974, *10,* 305–320.

Selye, H. (Ed.) *Guide to Stress Research.* Vol. 1. New York: Van Nostrand Reinhold, 1980.

Shanas, E. "Social Myth as Hypotheses: The Case of Family Relations of Old People." *The Gerontologist,* 1979, *19,* 3–10.

Spanier, G. B., and Casto, R. F. "Adjustment to Separation and Divorce: An Analysis of 50 Case Studies." *Journal of Divorce,* 1979, *2,* 241–253.

Spicer, J., and Hampe, G. "Kinship Interaction After Divorce." *Journal of Marriage and the Family,* 1975, *28,* 113–119.

Strodtbeck, F. L. "Husband-Wife Interaction Over Revealed Differences." *American Sociological Review,* 1951, *16,* 468–473.

Tessman, L. H. *Children of Parting Parents.* New York: Harper & Row, 1978.

Venters, M. *Chronic Childhood Illness, Disability and Familial Coping: The Case of Cystic Fibrosis.* Unpublished doctoral dissertation, University of Minnesota, St. Paul, 1979.

Wallerstein, J. S., and Kelly, J. B. *Surviving the Breakup. How Children and Parents Cope with Divorce.* New York: Basic Books, 1980.

Weiss, R. *Marital Separation.* New York: Basic Books, 1975.

Westman, J. D., Cline, D. W., Swift, W. J., and Kramer, D. A. "The Role of Child Psychiatry in Divorce." *Archives of General Psychiatry,* 1970, *23,* 416–420.

33

Wolkind, W., and Rutter, M. "Children Who Have Been 'in-care'—An Epidemiological Study." *Journal of Child Psychology and Psychiatry and Applied Disciplines*, 1973, *14*, 97–105.

E. Mavis Hetherington is professor of psychology at the University of Virginia, president of the Society for Research in Child Development, a past president of the Developmental Division of the American Psychological Association, and past editor of Child Development. *She is well known for her research and writing in the area of child development, particularly on the topic of divorce, one-parent families, and remarriage.*

The impact of marital discord on children's development is discussed in terms of models, methodology, results, and future required research.

Marital Discord and Children: Problems, Strategies, Methodologies, and Results

K. Daniel O'Leary

In Chapter One, Hetherington cautioned against becoming too attached to methods of research. I think this fierce attachment is true of those of us who use observational methodology in clinical/developmental research. I spent approximately ten years in observational work; a large portion of that was spent on methodological problems, particularly observer drift, shift, drop; reactivity in classrooms; and various types of reliability estimates that one can make (O'Leary and Johnson, 1979). Now I agree with Hetherington that we need to guard against focusing on molecular units of behavior without placing reasonable constructs upon those units. This fault was true of observations made in the classroom by researchers like Becker, Bijou, and myself. It was also true of Patterson and other investigators who did observational work in the home. The example given by Hetheringon of Gottman's work which relates to marital research, has the same problem. For example, the impact of

Part of the material presented here is the result of a collaborative effort with Robert Emery and Beatrice Porter (Porter and O'Leary, 1980; Emery, 1982), and also the result of a paper presented to a pediatric association in New Orleans (O'Leary and Emery, 1983). Mary Samios and Ernest Jouriles provided helpful editorial commentary.

A. Doyle, D. Gold, D. S. Moskowitz (Eds.). *Children in Families Under Stress.*
New Directions for Child Development, no. 24. San Francisco: Jossey-Bass, June 1984.

an observational code for marital interaction that takes twenty-eight hours to utilize for one hour of videotape interaction (Gottman and others, 1977) is of necessity limited, except for some possible theoretical interest for a small group of researchers. Such complex codes take weeks to develop, yet finally can be used only by the creators, their students, and typically one other research team. One has to ask what the real phenomena of interest are, and if there is a way of getting at those phenomena that is less costly and attunes the researcher more to the construct than to the many molecular units of behavior.

When research in the area of marital discord and the association between marital discord and childhood problems is examined, as in the area of stress, one finds that many methods have been used, involving many researchers from different disciplines. In fact, although I have warned against getting too attached to a particular method and one's own means of obtaining data, probably in this particular area there needs to be a greater emphasis on methodological concerns. In this chapter I will give a general introduction about why this area is of interest; then I will discuss the results of some research on marital–child interactions based on clinical samples and some of the problems inherent in that body of research. In addition, I will describe the results of research on marital–child interaction with nonclinic samples. Finally, I will describe some of the directions which I think researchers are taking toward answering some substantive as well as methodological questions.

Introduction: Marital Discord and Childhood Problems

Almost all workers in the mental health field assume that there is some type of interaction between marital discord and childhood problems. As early as 1944, Baruch and Wilcox reviewed the clinical literature and suggested, "There is a relationship between marital disharmony of the parents and the maladjustment in the child's personality and behavioral manifestations" (1944, p. 281). Essentially, psychodynamic behavior and family systems therapists assert that there is some association between marital and childhood problems. Interestingly enough, the behavior therapists have been the last actually to examine the larger system.

The issue of marital problems is addressed repeatedly in the media, with vivid depictions of what happens to both parents and children as a result of such discord. Unfortunately, while publicity on the phenomena is widespread, convincing research data is relatively scarce.

It is certainly possible that the association between marital and childhood problems can go both ways: That is, in addition to marital problems influencing childhood problems, childhood problems can influence marital problems (see Chapter Four). Researchers like Bell (1979), Lerner and Spanier (1978), and Margolin (1981) have discussed this issue at some length. However, one piece of data from a study of general populations of school children—that is, nonclinical populations—is worth describing here. In that study, the probability of having a discordant marriage, given a child with psychological problems, was less than the probability of having a child with psychological problems given a discordant marriage (Emery and O'Leary, 1983). Certainly marital problems do not always cause childhood problems, but at least in this study, with a sample of 152 children and their parents, the causal direction did appear to go from marital to childhood problems. Unfortunately, there is relatively little data that examines the situation the other way, except for studies with children who have physical handicaps. I have decided not to review that literature because I do not think it is especially germane to emotional problems of children. In terms of the association between marital and childhood problems in the framework of a general stressor (see Chapters One and Five), I suggest that, for studying children with emotional and behavioral problems, interactive models will be the models of the future. However, in this chapter I will discuss the association between marital discord and childhood problems, looking largely at marital interactions as they affect child behavior.

I became interested in the phenomenon during an evaluation of the effects of behavioral treatment for aggressive children in a project that involved consultation with parents, teachers, and the children themselves over a four-to-six-month period. Ron Kent, Lisa Serbin, I, and a number of others who were therapists on the project showed that behavioral interventions with aggressive second-, third-, and fourth-grade boys were effective (Kent and O'Leary, 1976, 1977). Further, we showed some maintenance of behavior nine months after the intervention and after there was no longer any contact with the therapist. Still, significant regression in a number of the children was also observed. We felt the regression was due to deterioration in a number of the parental dyads. Specifically, it appeared that mothers were not given enough support for the continued use of praise and the minimizing of reprimands and threats. They were also not supported for providing academic and tutorial help for their children. Under these conditions, the mothers became frustrated and often simply vacillated or stopped their supportive efforts with the child.

Who provides the support in changing their behavior with those children? In the late 1960s researchers such as Patterson said that the change in the child's behavior is generally sufficiently reinforcing to maintain a parent's behavior (Patterson and Reid, 1970). Then, some interesting reports appeared in the literature by researchers using tangible reinforcers to motivate parents—for example, a fee reduction for compliance with the program, a salary for parents who produce change in their child's behavior, a ticket to the hairdresser, or football game tickets (Reid and Hendricks, 1973). Essentially these researchers carried the reinforcement mode to the extreme because they saw that a change in the child's behavior alone was not enough to maintain parental compliance with the program. An alternative, however, is to think about ways of reinforcing the mother for dealing with the child, and also to look at the family system, which often appeared to be deteriorating. Some particular types of deterioration, other than the father not supporting the mother, were, for example, that the father would actually sabotage the mother in her efforts with the child. In many instances the parents were also providing aggressive, uncooperative models for the child. Sometimes, for instance, the child would actually pick up on the anxiety of the parent about the marital situation.

So, before providing any data, I will ask: Do observations like the one just made regarding deterioration in a child's behavior, apparently due to changes in parental behavior, change our clinical behavior? I believe they have influenced mine significantly, both from a clinical and research standpoint. About six years ago, for example, I saw an eleven-year-old boy whose mother reported that he was basically an uncooperative, noncompliant child who cursed and hit his brother frequently. The mother reported to me that she was now taking medication for high blood pressure. On the second visit, I found that one of the factors disturbing her was that her husband did not come home very early at night, and he often was out drinking. On the third or fourth occasion, I also found that the drinking involved infidelity and that there were relatively vituperative fights between the mother and the father.

The father was considering placement of his son in a local residential facility. I told the father that I thought such a decision was highly premature, and that I did not even want to see the boy until I had talked with both parents at some length. I told the father, "The reason I don't want to see your boy is because it's fairly obvious to me that you are providing the very model of the aggressive behavior you are attempting to get me to change, especially in your interactions with your wife." I asked them to go home and think about it for a week, then to give me a call if they wanted to come in. Fortunately, they did choose to come in, and the father and the mother were willing to address their significant marital discord. The father curtailed his drinking significantly, and I was able to see both the parents and the boy. The family's situation improved markedly, and I know that the boy has continued to make very significant progress in junior high school.

But that is a clinical example. The reader may ask, "Where's the real evidence?" There are few data dealing with the question I just described— that is, When there are both serious marital and child problems, should the child or the marital problems be treated first? A family systems person would say that the issue is irrelevant. However, I believe the question is worth attempting to answer empirically. Clark and Baker (1979) did provide some support for the idea that marital discord mitigates treatment effects with children. But in studies by Oltmanns, Broderick, and myself in 1977, with a sample of about 60 children, no evidence was found that marital discord mitigated behavioral treatment outcome. I do not quite believe this result; I would say instead that the methods used in this study may have failed. I would therefore like to examine this issue, not in regard to treatment outcome and the mitigating effect of treatment by marital problems, but simply by the association between marital and child problems, with clinic and nonclinic samples.

Marital Discord and Child Problems in Clinic Samples

The studies that follow were chosen because they are methodologically sound. Johnson and Lobitz (1974) studied a sample of seventeen couples who had taken their children to the Oregon clinic for "active behavioral problems," that is, the children were essentially problems. It was a small sample, but it was also one of the few studies in this area that utilized some observational as well as self-report data. The well-accepted measure of marital discord, the Locke-Wallace Marital Adjustment Test (Locke and Wallace, 1959), was used and the documentation of observational data was excellent. Johnson and Lobitz found a correlation of .45 between the Locke-Wallace Marital Adjustment Test and an observational measure of childhood problems taken on five occasions prior to the evening meal. They also found a significant association between marital discord and parental negativity toward the child.

Rutter (1970) assessed the relationship between marital discord and childhood psychopathology in a representative sample of all families living in a particular geographic area, in which one or both of the parents had been newly referred to a psychiatric clinic and had a child less than fifteen years of age. Again, this was a clinic sample, at least as defined by the parents. Rutter's study merits a fairly detailed description because he actually had more data than most other researchers. He had interview data to assess marital discord, a behavioral questionnaire completed by teachers to assess whether problem children were "behaviorally deviant," and individual clinical diagnoses made on the basis of interview data and on teacher questionnaires. In the sample of 250 parents referred to a psychiatric clinic, there was a greater likelihood of a male child being judged antisocial if the parents had poor marriages than if the parents had good marriages. No association was found for girls. Neurosis of the parents was not associated with marital discord in either boys or girls.

The Rutter study is important for several reasons. It was one of the first to find the differential association between marital discord and childhood problems for boys and girls. In addition, it also found that the clinical characteristics of the parent disorder were largely unrelated to the child's problems, except in the case of boys where antisocial personality types tended to have children with problems. Also of interest is a lengthy discussion of the reasons for the possible sex difference in response to family stress. Rutter believed that one of the reasons for this differential association is a sex-linked susceptibility both to psychological and biological stresses (Rutter, in press). He feels that marital discord is no different than any other problem that boys face. In essence he says that boys get "the short end of the stick" from birth to death, at birth being less likely to survive, and when later required to deal with psychological trauma, less capable of coping with it than girls are.

In our own studies at Stony Brook (O'Leary and others, 1983), we have looked at the association between marital discord and childhood problems using the Locke-Wallace Marital Adjustment Test as a barometer of marital discord and the Peterson-Quay Behavior Problem Check List as an indication of various behavior problems (Quay and Peterson, 1979).

Locke-Wallace test scores remain stable over a two-and-a-half-year period, (Kimmel and Van der veen, 1974). All couples have a two-hour interview as they enter our marital clinic, in which they are given a measure of marital communication (Navran, 1967) and a commitment index (Broderick and O'Leary, 1983). We assess feelings that are felt toward the other person but are not necessarily spoken (O'Leary and others, 1983). For example, on the measure of positive feelings toward a spouse, they rate how they feel toward a spouse on such items as "Hearing my spouse's voice on the phone makes me feel...," "When my spouse walks in the room he/she makes me feel...." Finally, we examine daily behavioral interactions (Vincent, 1972). We found that the Locke-Wallace correlated .52 with the commitment index and .88 with the measure of positive feelings toward a spouse.

Let me add a reason to be interested in such affective responses. I saw an attorney and his wife a few years ago. The wife was essentially willing to do almost anything to make her husband happy. I saw them for about five sessions, and the wife changed in a number of ways. It was not the case that the wife also wanted him to change in a number of ways; she was changing in a fashion to please her husband in every way that she felt she could. Her husband felt she was materialistic. He said that she was interested in redecorating the house every few years, she did not read a newspaper, she was not aware of her environment, that she was basically "uptight." I did not know until the sixth session that he was involved with somebody else. But because the man cared for his wife in a certain way, he called me with some concern. He said, "I really feel guilty because she is doing everything possible to change her behavior but I simply do not love my wife." In brief, he eventually divorced his wife and married the woman he was dating.

Because of cases like this, we try to assess feelings that are held toward a spouse but are not necessarily told to them. We wanted to know whether such feelings predict outcome in therapy. Unfortunately, they do not appear to for men, even though the measure we used is reliable and reasonably valid. On the other hand, this measure does predict women's response in therapy (Turkewitz and O'Leary, 1981). If the women have negative feelings toward their husbands at the beginning of therapy, this lack of positive affect is negatively related to our success with therapy across a six-month period with couples.

We assessed the relationship between marital and childhood problems in six different studies. With regard to clinic studies, we find that there is an association between marital problems and childhood problems, with correlations ranging generally in the realm of .30 to .40 for boys, particularly for conduct problems. However, like Rutter, we do not find a very consistent association between marital problems and childhood difficulties for girls. Rutter's research team and our group have found this differential association of marital discord for boys and girls, and Hetherington (Chapter One) also reported it from a somewhat different literature, that is, the literature on the impact of divorce on children.

We have been interested in why this differential association might exist. There are a number of hypotheses. We felt that displays of hostility in front of the children, especially by the father, might be an important factor. However, we have not seen greater hostility by parents in front of boys, at least as reported by parents or by children (Porter and O'Leary, 1980). However, I feel we were wrong in looking at a measure of hostility that reflected the extent to which the father and mother displayed aggressive and hostile behavior in front of the clinic-referred child. Because of our concern about having a measure with demonstrable reliability of judgment, our questions were phrased in such a manner that the father and mother indicated the extent to which they did certain things together and in front of the clinic-referred child. Indeed, we were able to obtain reasonable interrater agreement between parents. But we are now interested in assessing whether either the mother or father reports displays of hostile behavior toward one another and what kind of modeling and coping effects we observe in the children when they witness parental behavior.

A second possible explanation for the differential association between marital problems and the behavior problems of boys and girls is differential awareness. Nevertheless, we have found that boys and girls have relatively accurate perceptions of their parents' marital adjustment, with correlations of about .50 for both sexes (Emery and O'Leary, 1982). Finally, it is possible that mothers from discordant marriages use more negative discipline practices with boys than with girls. In this vein, we often hear a mother report that her son's detestable behavior seems "just like the old man," especially in the case of adolescents, when the boy develops and begins to look physically like his father. Many mothers say, "I watch him as he walks down a room or walks in the door; he's got that same swagger his old man has. He swears like he does, and he throws his clothes around just like his father. When he looks and acts like his father, I just feel like hitting him." There is conflicting evidence regarding documentation for such displacement of wives' negative feelings toward their husbands onto their male children (Bond, 1983; Porter, 1981), but I think this issue is worthy of serious research attention.

Marital Discord and Childhood Problems in Nonclinic Samples

The rationale for considering the possible displacement of negative feelings of parents toward their spouses onto their children is based on nonclinic findings. In nonclinic findings, there is a greater association between marital discord and childhood problems when parents' reports of child behavior are used rather than teachers' reports (Emery and O'Leary, 1983). That is, when an independent observation of child behavior outside the family is included in studies with clinic samples, there is less of an association between marital discord and childhood problems. This may be a methodological issue; mothers may see their sons more negatively than outside observers, thus introducing a negative bias, into the self-reports. Alternatively, the association found between parental reports of marital discord and childhood behavior problems may be due in part to a negative set the parent has as he or she completes these questionnaires. However, clinically, it is our impression that the conduct-problem child is more likely to reveal very gross behaviors at home than at school, unless there is severe punishment for such behavior at home. A child will swear, act out, and display the full range of conduct problem behaviors at home, but this same child may not be a serious behavior problem at school. If such were the case, a greater association between marital and child problems might exist because of a greater variance in child problems at home than at school. With regard to the methodological issue of how to assess this association, we need to be attuned to the possibility of response bias by the parents and the need for some independent evaluation of the child's behavior.

In addition to the need for independent assessments of child behavior, we need more specific breakdowns of the types of childhood problems assessed. For example, enuresis does not appear to be associated with marital discord, whereas encopresis does (Doleys, 1981). It would be worthwhile to look at other types of specific childhood problems. Moreover, we need measurement of other variables in addition to marital discord as predictors or moderators of childhood problems. For example, variables such as a close relationship with the parents or a child's support by a teacher may moderate the association between marital discord and childhood problems. I think there are two directions to take in future research — to look at much larger samples of children and to look at multiple predictors and moderators, and we need multicenter studies to look at various types of childhood problems developmentally. That is, very large samples are needed in order to be able to study moderators and predictors as they operate together in boys and girls at different ages.

Second, however, it would also be worthwhile to conduct small-sample studies to examine certain problems intensively. For example, while the association between marital problems and behavior problems of girls has not been documented, there is likely to be some impact of marital problems on girls. The measures are probably not appropriate or sufficiently sensitive. We have examined means and standard deviations to assess whether boys and girls differ on the various factor scores from the Peterson-Quay Behavior Problem Checklist. Often they do not (Porter and O'Leary, 1980). However, one could study groups of girls where there is intense marital discord, and use the interview method to derive initial hypotheses to be explored later in studies with multiple measures. Some observations could be made and discussions could be held with the parent to assess how these girls cope with marital discord.

Regarding other methodological problems, some analyses of the long-term effects of marital discord and the types of discord are needed. For example, my main research area is physical abuse, and one of the factors that we and others see as the biggest predictor of physical abuse is whether the abuser saw his father hit his mother or whether he was repeatedly hit as a child (Rosenbaum and O'Leary, 1981; Curley and O'Leary, 1980). It might be possible to mitigate the long-term and short-term effects of marital discord with reference to certain types of clinical problems.

There is another level at which it is worthwhile discussing the issue of discord and divorce at this time. Obviously, marital discord, separation, and divorce have some bad effects in the family. However, when the magnitude of the correlations are examined, one has to say optimistically that the effects in nonclinic populations appear relatively small. In the final part of this chapter I will summarize several studies and then come to some general conclusion about the nonclinic samples. The first two I will describe are those by Rutter and his colleagues (Rutter and others, 1975; 1976). The first dealt with ten-year-olds, the second with the same group of children four years later. Essentially, with the same sample of 250 children, Rutter showed various associations between marital discord and childhood psychopathology if he broke the marital population down with regard to severe, moderate, and minimal problems or no discord. Whitehead (1979), with a sample of 2,775 seven-year-old first-born children, one of the largest samples yet, also found some association between marital and childhood problems. Unfortunately, from the way the data were presented, we cannot derive the magnitude of the association, but given the sample size and the probability levels reported the association was not strong. In a nonclinic sample of 125 elementary school pupils, Emery (1981) found significant associations between marital discord and parental ratings of childhood problems for boys, with correlations ranging generally between 0.15 and 0.25. There were similar associations for girls. In a study in Johannesburg, South Africa, with another 250 nonclinic elementary school children, we achieved essentially the same result. There was an association between marital discord and childhood problems for boys of about .20; there were few significant findings for the girls (Barling and O'Leary, 1983).

The general conclusion to be drawn from nonclinic studies is that, with small samples of less than 50, there is little association between marital discord and child problems. With larger samples of over 100, a significant association can be found. But the issue that remains is the meaning of that association in which the magnitude is small. At the 1981 American Psychological Association meeting in Los Angeles, Don Baer said in his polite, wry way, that one can look at marital discord, intelligence, and socioeconomic status, but what do they indicate? He claims that these variables are marker variables, which indicate that something is wrong somewhere else. He asked several of us on the panel: "Why don't you look at the parental discipline practices as mediated possibly by the marital discord? Why don't you look at support given by one

44

parent and the other? Why don't you look at various events that can happen in a more functional way?" I think his point is well taken, and that an association exists between marital discord and childhood problems. There is a differential association for boys and girls, but the overall view has not been put together yet in the examination of many variables simultaneously — for example, discipline practices, discord, and support. Unfortunately, such research takes gigantic samples.

In particular, one of the factors that I soon hope to examine is the shielding of children from marital discord by fathers and mothers. We should also study the modeling of aggression displayed by the father and directed at the mother, because if we intensively study boys who are aggressive, we will see that they model some of their father's aggressive behaviors. Girls also see their fathers acting aggressively toward their mothers, and we can ask what their coping mechanisms are. The study of girls and how they cope with family stresses is a neglected area. As was aptly pointed out by Hetherington in Chapter One, what girls may be doing can be quite different at certain stages of their life, for example, in the latency period or as teenagers. We have to break the children's ages down into units that can be handled reasonably.

To summarize, the association between marital discord and divorce is greater for boys than for girls. However, we need to study more intensively what happens to girls, as they have been relatively neglected in this research area. In a positive sense, however, remember that many people have somehow coped with divorce and separation. The magnitude of the association between discord and child problems is relatively small for nonclinic populations. We need to examine how children positively cope with separation and divorce, or how they positively cope with discord when it continues for years. Many couples remain discordant throughout their lifetime without ever getting divorced, and their children repeatedly have to cope with that stress. We need to study how children successfully cope with the negative vicissitudes of marital life.

References

Baer, D. M. "Comments on the Symposium." *The Relationship Between Marital and Child Adjustment: Empirical Findings.* Annual meeting of the American Psychological Association, Los Angeles, Calif., 1981.
Barling, J., and O'Leary, K. D. "Relationships Between Marital and Childhood Problems in South Africa." Unpublished manuscript. State University of New York: Stony Brook, 1983.
Baruch, D. W., and Wilcox, J. A. "A Study of Sex Differences in Preschool Children's Adjustment Coexistent with Interpersonal Tensions." *The Journal of Genetic Psychology,* 1944, *64,* 281–303.
Bell, R. Q. "Parent, Child, and Reciprocal Influences." *American Psychologist,* 1979, *34,* 821–826.
Bond, C. R. "The Relationships Between Marital Distress and Child Behavior Problems, Maternal Personal Adjustment, Maternal Personality, and Maternal Parenting Behavior." Unpublished doctoral dissertation, University of British Columbia, Vancouver, 1983.

Broderick, J. E., and O'Leary, K. D. "Contributions of Behavior and Attitudes to Marital Satisfaction." Unpublished manuscript, State University of New York, Stony Brook, 1983.

Clark, D. B., and Baker, B. L. "Training of Developmentally Disabled Children: Prediction of Follow-up Outcome." Paper presented at the annual meeting of the American Psychological Association, New York, September 1979.

Curley, A. D., and O'Leary, K. D. "Psychological Correlates of Spouse Abuse." Paper presented to the annual meeting of the Association for the Advancement of Behavior Therapy, New York, November 1980.

Doleys, D. "Encopresis." In J. M. Ferguson and C. B. Taylor (Eds.) *The Comprehensive Handbook of Behavioral Medicine, 2.* Jamaica, N.Y.: Spectrum, 1981.

Emery, R. E. "Marital Discord and Child Behavior Problems in a Nonclinic Sample." Unpublished manuscript, University of Virginia, 1981.

Emery, R. E. "Marital Turmoil: Interpersonal Conflict and the Children of Discord and Divorce." *Psychological Bulletin,* 1982, *92,* 310-330.

Emery, R. E., and O'Leary, K. D. "Children's Perceptions of Marital Discord and Behavior Problems of Boys and Girls." *Journal of Abnormal Child Psychology,* 1982, *10,* 11-24.

Emery, R. E., and O'Leary, K. D. "Marital Discord and Child Behavior Problems in a Normative Sample." Unpublished manuscript, University of Virginia, Charlottesville, 1983.

Gottman, J., Markmann, H., and Notarius, C. "The Topography of Marital Conflict: A Sequential Analysis of Verbal and Nonverbal Behavior." *Journal of Marriage and the Family,* 1977, *39,* 461-477.

Johnson, S. M., and Lobitz, C. K. "The Personal and Marital Adjustment of Parents as Related to Observed Child Deviance and Parenting Behavior." *Journal of Abnormal Child Psychology,* 1974, *2,* 193-207.

Kent, R. W., and O'Leary, K. D. "A Controlled Evaluation of Behavior Modification with Conduct Problem Children." *Journal of Consulting Clinical Psychology,* 1976, *44,* 586-596.

Kent, R. M., and O'Leary, K. D. "Treatment of Conduct Problem Children: B. A. and/or Ph.D. Therapists." *Behavior Therapy,* 1977, *8,* 653-658.

Kimmel, D. C., and Van der veen, F. "Factors of Marital Adjustment in Locke's Marital Adjustment Test." *Journal of Marriage and the Family,* 1974, *36,* 57-63.

Lerner, R. M., and Spanier, G. B. *Child Influences on Marital and Family Interaction: A Life-Span Perspective.* New York: Academic Press, 1978.

Locke, H. J., and Wallace, K. M. "Short Marital Adjustment and Prediction Tests: Their Reliability and Validity." *Marriage and Family Living,* 1959, *21,* 251-255.

Margolin, G. "The Reciprocal Relationship Between Marital and Child Problems." In J. P. Vincent (Ed.), *Advances in Family Intervention, Assessment and Theory: An Annual Compilation of Research.* Greenwich, Conn.: Jai, 1981.

Navran, L. "Communication and Adjustment in Marriage." *Family Process,* 1967, *6,* 173-184.

O'Leary, K. D., and Johnson, S. B. "Assessment of Psychopathological Disorders in Children." In H. C. Quay and J. S. Werry (Eds.), *Psychopathological Disorders of Childhood.* (2nd ed.) New York: Wiley, 1979.

O'Leary, K. D., Fincham, F., and Turkewitz, H. "Assessment of Positive Feelings Toward Spouses." *Journal of Consulting and Clinical Psychology,* 1983, *51,* 949-951.

O'Leary, K. D., and Emery, R. E. "Marital Discord and Child Behavior Problems." In M. D. Levine and P. Satz (Eds.), *Developmental Variation and Dysfunction.* New York: Academic Press, 1983.

Oltmanns, T. F., Broderick, J. E., and O'Leary, K. D. "Marital Adjustment and the Efficacy of Behavior Therapy with Children." *Journal of Consulting and Clinical Psychology,* 1977, *45,* 724-729.

46

Patterson, G. R., and Reid, J. B. "Reciprocity and Coercion: Two Facets of Social Systems." In C. Neuringer and J. L. Michael (Eds.), *Behavior Modification in Clinical Psychology.* New York: Appleton-Century-Crofts, 1970.

Porter, B. "Parent Behavior and Feelings in Distressed and Nondistressed Marriages." Unpublished doctoral dissertation, State University of New York, Stony Brook, 1981.

Porter, B., and O'Leary, K. D. "Types of Marital Discord and Child Behavior Problems." *Journal of Abnormal Child Psychology,* 1980, *8,* 287–295.

Quay, H. C., and Peterson, D. R. *Manual for the Behavior Problem Checklist.* Available from Dr. D. R. Peterson, 39 North Fifth, Highland Park, New Jersey 08904, 1979.

Reid, J. B., and Hendricks, A. F. C. J. "Preliminary Analysis of the Effectiveness of Direct Home Intervention for the Treatment of Predelinquent Boys Who Steal." In L. Hamerlynck, L. Handy. and E. Mash (Eds.), *Behavior Change: Methodology, Concepts, and Practice.* Champaign, Ill.: Research Press, 1973.

Rosenbaum, A., and O'Leary, K. D. "Marital Violence: Characteristics of Abusive Couples." *Journal of Consulting and Clinical Psychology,* 1981, *49,* 63–71.

Rutter, M. "Sex Differences in Children's Response to Family Stress." In E. J. Anthony and C. Koupernik (Eds.), *The Child in His Family.* New York: Wiley, 1970.

Rutter, M. "The Family, the Child and the School." In M. D. Levine and P. Satz (Eds.), *Developmental Variation and Dysfunction.* New York: Academic Press, in press.

Rutter, M., Graham, P., Chadwick, O. F. D., and Yule, W. "Adolescent Turmoil: Fact or Fiction." *Journal of Child Psychology and Psychiatry,* 1976, *17,* 35–56.

Rutter, M., Yule, B., Quinton, D., Rowlands, O., Yule, W., and Berger, M. "Attainment and Adjustment in Two Geographic Areas. Some Accounting for Area Differences." *British Journal of Psychiatry,* 1975, *126,* 520–523.

Turkewitz, H., and O'Leary, K. D. "A Comparative Outcome Study of Behavioral Marital Therapy and Communication Therapy." *Journal of Marital and Family Therapy,* 1981, *7,* 159–169.

Vincent, J. "The Relationship of Sex, Level of Intimacy and Level of Marital Distress to Problem-Solving Behavior and Exchange of Social Reinforcement." Unpublished doctoral dissertation, University of Oregon, Eugene, 1972.

Whitehead, L. "Sex Differences in Children's Responses to Family Stress." *Journal of Child Psychology and Psychiatry,* 1979, *20,* 247–254.

K. Daniel O'Leary is professor of psychology at the State University of New York in Stony Brook, and was listed as one of the world's one hundred most cited psychologists (American Psychologist, December 1978). *He coauthored* Behavior Therapy: Application and Outcome *(Prentice-Hall, 1977),* Classroom Management *(Pergamon Press, 1979), and* Principles of Behavior Therapy *(Prentice-Hall, 1980). Recently he published* Coping with Behavior Problems of Children *(Horizon Press, 1984). He is also a practicing therapist and is president of the Association for the Advancement of Behavior Therapy.*

*Parents with a high level of communication deviance and negative
expressed emotion or emotional overinvolvment have children who
are at greater risk for schizophrenia.*

Family Affect and Communication Related to Schizophrenia

Michael J. Goldstein

A number of factors in recent years have rekindled interest in the role of the
family in schizophrenia. First, the trend toward deinstitutionalization of
schizophrenic patients and the emphasis on community-based care often
return patients to a family environment. Examination of these environments
has revealed that some families cope well with this newly assigned caretaker
role, but that many experience considerable difficulty reabsorbing a member
who frequently manifests a number of residual symptoms. Concern with the
nature of the family environment and its impact on the newly discharged
schizophrenic patient has revived interest in the family's role in schizophrenia
in general.

Second, the studies by Brown and others (1972) and later by Vaughn
and Leff (1976) in Great Britain provide empirical evidence that negative
aspects of the family environment can be specified and measured with standardized procedures. Their work on expressed emotion (EE) reveals that

The research reported in this paper was supported by grants MH08744 and
MH30911 from the U.S. National Institute of Mental Health. Special appreciation is
due Jeri A. Doane, Julia M. Lewis, and David Miklowtiz for their generous contributions to the research program and for permitting aspects of their data to be reproduced
in this paper. Ian Falloon has been most generous in sharing data from his intervention
projects with families containing schizophrenic offspring.

A. Doyle, D. Gold, D. S. Moskowitz (Eds.). *Children in Families Under Stress.*
New Directions for Child Development, no. 24. San Francisco: Jossey-Bass, June 1984.

indexes of overinvolvement, hostility, and critical comments made by the patient's relatives (usually the parents) in the course of a standardized interview administered about the time the patient was admitted to the hospital — the Camberwell Family Interview (CFI) — possessed powerful prognostic information concerning the likelihood of relapse over a nine-month follow-up period. The EE variable, assumed to reflect ongoing intrafamilial attitudes and processes, suggests a particular sensitivity of the schizophrenic patient to discriminable attitudes of the family emotional environment.

Third, the past ten years have witnessed a number of research programs concerned with the developmental antecedents of adult schizophrenia (Garmezy, 1974). These studies have focused on populations believed to be at greater than average risk for schizophrenia, which are identified and studied prior to the onset of the clinical form of the disorder. These samples are followed from some earlier life period until they enter the risk period for adult schizophrenia. Several of these projects have included measures of intrafamilial characteristics in their early assessments so that the value of familial predictors of the onset of a schizophrenic episode can be evaluated. These studies have involved a high level of sophistication in the assessment of family relationships and more precise specification of family parameters than was the case in earlier family research. Some of the variables measured have been derived from these earlier studies of families containing adult schizophrenic offspring, for example, the Singer-Wynne concept of communication deviance (Singer, 1967; Wynne and others, 1976). Others have been derived from the work on family factors associated with the course of schizophrenia, factors involving interpersonal derivatives of the expressed emotion dimensions.

It is sometimes implied that current interest in the family's role in the course of schizophrenia has little bearing on etiological issues. In one sense, this is entirely correct. However, in another sense it represents a false distinction between family factors that are associated with onset and those that relate to course. Both types of research deal with issues of life course — one from an ostensibly illness-free period to the first appearance of a schizophrenic disorder and the other from a period of overt, symptomatic manifestation of the disorder to a relatively illness-free period. While this is an issue ultimately answered by empirical data, it is difficult for the author to view family life as so discontinuous across the life span that those attributes of the family environment related to the onset of schizophrenia do not overlap with those associated with its differential course following an initial episode.

Family Factors Related to the Onset of Schizophrenia

Are there definable aspects of intrafamilial relationships that precede the onset to schizophrenia or its prodromal signs? A study carried out at the University of California, Los Angeles by my research group (Doane and others, 1981) provides evidence that family attributes measured during adolescence are associated with the subsequent presence of schizophrenia or schizophrenia-related disorders in the offspring once they enter young adulthood. A cohort of sixty-five non-psychotically disturbed adolescents and their families participated in this prospective longitudinal study. At the time of the first five-year follow-up, a measure of communication deviance, as defined by the Singer-Wynne criteria, was available for thirty-seven of the cases and predicted the presence of disorders on the extended schizophrenia spectrum (Wender and others, 1968). Very briefly, a measure of parental communication deviance (CD) developed by Jones (1977) was obtained from Thematic Apperception Test (TAT) data obtained at the time of the original assessment. Examples of this measure include lack of commitment to ideas or precepts, unclear or idiosyncratic communication of themes or ideas, language anomalies, disruptive speech, and closure problems. Offspring of parents with high levels of parental CD were more likely to have schizophrenia or schizophrenia-spectrum disorders at the time of the first five-year follow-up. Low CD in the parents was a good predictor of a relatively benign, non-schizophrenia spectrum disorder. However, a number of false-positive errors occurred in which several cases with relatively benign outcomes also had parents with high CD. Thus, the CD index alone did not allow precise identification of those cases destined to develop schizophrenic and related disorders.

Consequently, a measure similar to EE, affective style (AS), was used to determine whether this attribute would enhance the prediction of the onset of schizophrenia in this sample of disturbed adolencents. Certain key components of the affective style index (such as criticism, guilt inducement, and intrusiveness), derived from directly observed family interactions, can be construed as interpersonal analogues of certain dimensions of the EE construct. Doane and others (1981) found that when a measure of affective style — obtained from a modified Strodtbeck (1954) direct interaction task involving all family members — was added to the CD index, remarkably precise prediction resulted. For the same sample of thirty-seven cases, only cases whose parents exhibited both high CD and negative AS manifested schizophrenia-spectrum disorders at the five-year follow-up. While both of these parental characteristics were measured at least five years prior to the onset of overt schizophrenic symptomatology and, therefore, were clearly not reactive to the presence of psychosis in offspring, one cannot assume from these results that they play an etiological role in the development of schizophrenia. Data that will soon be available from the fifteen-year follow-up of these cases will provide even clearer evidence for the predictive value of these and other family characteristics.

Interactional Correlates of CD. The measure of communication deviance clearly serves as an important marker of parental attributes associated with subsequent schizophrenia-spectrum disorders in offspring. However, unlike the AS index, which is derived from directly observed interaction between parent and teenager, CD is based upon transactions between a parent and a tester during the administration of a projective test, the TAT. But what

50

does this index reveal about ongoing family interaction? Researchers from our group previously reported correlates of CD (Goldstein and others, 1978) which revealed that high-CD parents manifested significantly more non-acknowledging behavior in triadic interactions than parents classified as inter-mediate or low, particularly when responding to the offspring. Also, Lieber (1977) found that high-CD parents, when observed in a structured discussion of videotapes of their own triadic interaction, were less likely than other par-ents to use task-focusing comments when the discussion drifted from the requested structure. Both of these studies support the idea that high-CD parents, when involved in a three-way emotionally charged discussion with their disturbed teenager, have difficulty maintaining an effective focus of discussion.

A study by Lewis (1979) pursued this issue in more detail by examin-ing aspects of role structure, communication drift, and nonverbal behavior in triadic family discussions. Her role structure estimates were based on speaking patterns—who talks and who is the recipient of others' remarks. Using a pro-file approach, she characterized families as father-central, mother-central, dual-parental focus, or mixed. Father- and mother-central families feature one parent who is the primary speaker and recipient of the other two family member's remarks. Dual-parental focus characterizes a triadic interaction in which both parents are equally active and direct the majority of their com-ments to the teenager. In the mixed pattern, either the parents speak only to one another or one parent talks to the child, who in turn addresses another parent, who in turn addresses another speaker, a *ronde* of sorts. Lewis pre-dicted, based on research in families containing a schizophrenic offspring, that the father-central pattern would be less common in the high-CD family units. As Table 1 indicates, the prediction is confirmed, although the rates for high and intermediate CD groups are the same. In addition, other patterns are noted in high-CD family units, particularly a mother-central or dual-parental focus, role structures that are rarely noted in intermediate- or low-CD family

Table 1. Parental Role Structure versus Communication Deviance
(N = 47)*

Level of Communication Deviance	Father-Central	Mother-Central	Dual-Parental Focus	Mixed Patterns
Low	10	2	0	0
Intermediate	5	2	0	8
High	5	8	6	1

chi square = 30.96, p< .0001
*47 of 65 cases had both *CD* ratings and rateable interaction transcripts.
Source: Lewis and others, 1981.

units. Obviously, there is more heterogeneity in the role structure patterns of the high-CD than the other two CD groups, but a father-central focus occurs much less frequently than in low-CD families. The discrepancy between high- and low-CD families is particularly noteworthy for the mother-central and dual-parental focus family structures.

The heterogeneity in the high-CD groups may explain why previous attempts to compare families containing schizophrenic offspring with other groups on similar measures have produced a "now you see it, now you don't" pattern of results. These have all looked for a single pattern, such as maternal or paternal dominance, when Lewis' data (1979) suggest strongly that there may be a number of distorted role patterns in pre-schizophrenic families that are lost when simple averages are used to contrast groups. These data are also congruent with the observations of Lidz and others (1965), who observed a number of different role-structure patterns in their sample of families of schizophrenics, patterns which were all disordered in some way. It appears that, as with the data of Lidz and others, pre-schizophrenic families share a common feature of disordered communication and affective style, but vary in the precise formal organization in which these processes are expressed.

Lewis (1979) made further attempts to account for the heterogeneity in role patterns. She hypothesized that they may reflect different patterns of CD in the parents. The criteria developed by Jones for the high-CD classification utilized the multifactorial nature of the index. Jones (1977) found that when a single parent scored high (T score = 60) on Factor 2 (misperceptions) or 6 (major closure problems) the probability of schizophrenia in their offspring was high. Therefore, he classified a parental unit as high-CD if either parent manifested a high score on Factor 2 or 6 independently of the other parent's score. For the remaining CD factors, Jones found that T scores greater than 60 were required from both parents for the risk of schizophrenia in offspring to be high. Therefore, another group of parents in the University of California, Los Angeles sample were classified by Lewis as high-CD only when both parents manifested T scores above 60 on CD factors other than Factor 2 or 6.

Lewis (1979) next grouped the high-CD parents on the basis of the different criteria suggested by Jones for entry into the high-CD group (for example, single- or dual-parent requirement). In Table 2, close correspondence between these criteria and role structure pattern can be seen. When the father's CD was high on the basis of the 2–6 factor pattern (regardless of the mother's pattern), the father-central structural pattern can be observed; where the mother was classified as high-CD on the basis of the 2–6 pattern, a mother-central pattern can be seen; and when both parents manifested high-CD on the remaining factors, the dual parental-focus pattern is apparent. Thus, not only was Lewis able to demonstrate parallelism between CD criteria and role structure, but she found that the parent or parents who actually have the high-CD deficit are central in the triadic family discussion. Such parents are actively involved in family relationships and may, in fact, dominate the family environ-

Table 2. Parental Communication Deviance Inclusion Criteria
and Role Structure Pattern (*N* = 20)

	CD Factor		Role Structure	
Pattern		Father-Central	Dual-Parental Focus	Mother-Central
Father high (2, 6) *or* both parents (2, 6)		4	1	2
Both parents high (1, 3, 4, or 5)		0	4	2
Mother only high (2,6)		1	1	5

Source: Lewis, 1979.

ment. Were this not the case, a theoretical embarrassment would exist. If the high-CD parent was relatively inactive or ignored, then we would have difficulty explaining the mechanism by which the CD index translates into pathological family relationships. The notable activity level of the parent suggests that high-CD parents are very significant in setting the form and probably the intensity of family discussions.

To understand better what type of tone is set within these parental structures, Lewis investigated the two other dimensions of CD, communication drift and nonverbal affect display. Communication drift was measured with regard to two factors, adherence to the topic and expression of feelings. Failure to adhere to the topic was indexed by one of two patterns, drift from the assigned problem for discussion, or such rigid adherence to the defined topic that meaningful discussion was precluded. For sharing feelings, two parallel deviations were excessive outpouring of feelings or rigid suppression of all feelings. High-CD families generally avoided sharing feelings with each other and were more likely to show distorted communication of the assigned topic, but surprisingly enough, the tendency was toward rigid adherence to the topic rather than a drifting, disorganizing style. The relationship between CD and communication drift was not as sharp, however, as was noted for the previously mentioned role-structure measures.

When notable rigidity and avoidance of feelings were both observed, they were most commonly seen in father-central family units. This was an important difference between father-central families in the high- and low-CD groups. In the low-CD groups, high father activity was associated with clear communication and affect sharing. In the high-CD group, the same role structure was associated with rigid adherence to the topic and avoidance of affect sharing. Thus, in the high-CD families of this subgroup, paternal activity blocks rather than facilitates family communication. Simply categorizing families as father- or mother-central, as in prior family research, would lose this qualitative difference and lead to the erroneous conclusion that schizophrenic and non-schizophrenic families are similar.

The third correlate of CD explored by Lewis was nonverbal aspects of parental behavior noted during the triadic discussion. The components were eye contact, facial expression, and voice tone. Voice tone did not relate to the other nonverbal measures but did relate strongly to the Affective Style Index, which was derived from content analysis of verbal transcripts. The eye contact and facial expression measures were combined into profile groupings as follows: (1) Avoidant eye contact and rigid facial expression; (2) nonavoidant eye contact and rigid facial expression; and (3) nonavoidant eye contact and relaxed facial expression. In Table 3, high-CD is associated with parental avoidance of eye contact with the adolescent and a rigid unchanging facial expression, while the other CD groups show less avoidance behavior and emotional rigidity.

We can see that two broad constructs, CD and AS, are valuable in predicting offspring diagnostic status at the time of the five-year follow-up. Communication deviance, as measured by an individual projective test administered to the parents, clearly indexes more than its name would imply and reveals family units that generally lack in effective paternal participation, are poorly organized in dealing with emotional material, and show signs of marked interpersonal tension between parent and teenager. The affect measures, which are most parsimoniously thought of as measures of an affective evaluation of the teenager expressed in words and tone of voice, appear orthogonal or at least oblique to interpersonal correlates of the CD index. Further, they are an important ingredient in accounting for variation in early adult outcomes. Poorly organized and tense family structures lacking negative evaluative attitudes (criticism, guilt induction, or intrusiveness) do not contain early onset, definite or probable schizophrenia, or borderline personality disorders. Whether the eidence from the longer term follow-up supports this two-factor model or indicates that it may only be relevant for early onset cases remains to be seen.

Table 3. Nonverbal Behavior versus Communication Deviance ($n = 34$)*

Level of Communication Deviance	Nonverbal Behavior		
	Nonavoidant and relaxed	Nonavoidant and rigid	Avoidant and rigid
Low	8	0	2
Intermediate	2	6	1
High	2	4	9

chi square = 20.12, $p < .0005$

*Only 34 families had CD ratings and usable videotapes for rating facial expression and body position.

Source: Lewis and others, 1981.

Family Factors Associated with the Course of Schizophrenia

A second body of research that addresses the role of family factors in the course of schizophrenia, once it has been diagnosed, is in progress. As mentioned earlier, the work by Brown and others (1972) showed patients returning to a high-EE family environment were much more likely to relapse during the nine months following hospitalization. Vaughn and Leff (1976) replicated their initial findings and the combined data from these studies revealed the following relapse rates: 51 percent of the high-EE group had relapsed within nine months of hospital release versus 13 percent of the low-EE group (Leff, 1976).

While the EE work has been stimulating, it has raised as many questions as it has answered. Several important issues are currently being addressed in a number of studies: First, can this finding be replicated in other settings? A second issue concerns construct validity. Do people who display critical or overinvolved attitudes on the Camberwell Family Interview (CFI) also convey these attitudes during actual interactions with the patient? Third, are EE attitudes in family members independent of patient characteristics, such as premorbid status or quality or severity of symptomatology, as suggested by the original investigators? Fourth, how does EE relate to other familial attributes shown in previous research to be associated with families of schizophrenics, such as communication deviance? Finally, we do not yet know whether the relationship between EE and relapse rates is equally valid for other cultural or subcultural groups.

Replication Studies. A recent replication study by Vaughn and others (1982) at the University of California, Los Angeles and Camarillo State Hospital reports remarkably similar relapse rates for a sample of 54 schizophrenics of low- and high-EE families. These investigators found that 57 percent of the high-EE cases relapsed within nine months in contrast to only 17 percent of the low-EE group. Other replication studies are currently underway in this country as well as in Denmark, Great Britain, and India (Day, 1982).

Construct Validity Issues. While replication studies are important in any scientific endeavor, issues involving the validity of the findings are equally crucial. If we take EE, for example, we can ask what exactly this measure reflects. Presumably EE attitudes as conveyed to the interviewer during the CFI, are reflective and perhaps even characteristic of how the relative relates to the patient in the interpersonal situations and discussions of everyday life. However, this issue has not been put to empirical test. In short, does high-EE status indicate indiscriminable, characteristic negative interpersonal modes of relating to the patient, or does it reflect an attitudinal position not manifested in actual behavior?

Two recent studies provide indirect evidence for the construct validity of EE. Tarrier and others (1979) reported that in the home setting patients with low-EE and those with high-EE relatives both displayed a high degree of arousal, measured as a high frequency of spontaneous fluctuations in skin conductance, when the target relative was not present in the room. However, after the target relative had entered the room, the patients with low-EE relatives rapidly habituated while those with high-EE relatives did not. This finding was replicated in a recent report by Sturgeon and others (1981), who found very similar results. These studies suggest that there is something relatively more soothing or less noxious about the low-EE relatives. What the high-EE relatives do differently, however, remains unexamined.

An obvious hypothesis is that the high-EE relative behaves in a highly critical, hostile, or overinvolved fashion when interacting with the patient. The measure of AS cited previously (Doane and others, 1981) is being used to examine this question in two projects underway in Los Angeles. In a project directed by Falloon at the University of Southern California, forty high-EE families have been randomly assigned to family therapy or individual therapy (Falloon and others, 1981). Among the data collected are EE ratings of criticism, hostility, and overinvolvement derived from the CFI, and two directly observed family interaction tasks, similar in format to those used in the longitudinal study mentioned earlier (Doane and others, 1981). Preliminary analyses on a pilot sample of fifteen high- and fifteen low-EE families indicate that measures of Doane's affective style in the family discussion tasks are associated with corresponding attitudes conveyed during the CFI (see Figure 1). Note that the high-EE families have been subdivided into three groups, critical ($N = 4$), critical plus emotional overinvolvement (EOI) ($N = 3$), and EOI only ($N = 8$), based on the pattern manifested by the relative on the CFI. The results indicate that high-EE parents so designated because of an excess number of critical comments also use significantly more critical remarks in the direct interaction task, while those designated as high-EE because of noncritical but overinvolved attitudes (see Figure 2) display less criticism but significantly more intrusive remarks such as telling the patient how he or she thinks or feels and what motivates him or her. It is notable that subdividing the high-EE relatives into those who were predominantly critical, predominantly overinvolved, or those with both characteristics resulted in significant relationships to the affective style of the relatives' interaction with the patient. This strategy is in sharp contrast to the dichotomous categorization employed in the British predictive studies. It may be that the dichotomous grouping is sufficient for prediction of relapse, while further subcategorization of high-EE is more useful for analyzing its relationship to other variables.

EE Status and Patient Characteristics. Vaughn and Leff (1976) originally reported that high- or low-EE status of the relatives could not be explained by characteristics of the patients such as severe symptomatology or premorbid status. This area is being further explored in several ongoing research projects studying the impact of EE on the course of schizophrenia. A pilot analysis by Miklowitz (1981) of data from the Falloon study suggests this issue is more complex than originally suggested by Vaughn and Leff. Of

56

Figure 1. Number of Critical Statements Expressed in Direct
Interaction by Mothers in Different EE Subgroups

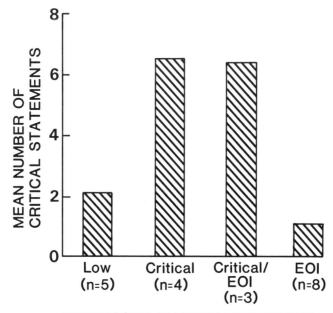

CRITICAL COMMENTS EXPRESSED IN
DIRECT INTERACTION BY MOTHERS
IN DIFFERENT EE SUBGROUPS

thirty-three cases, patients from families where the mothers displayed emotionally overinvolved attitudes on the CFI were rated as significantly poorer in
premorbid adjustment on the UCLA Social Attainment Scale (Goldstein,
1978) than cases in which mothers were highly critical or low-EE. These data
are presented in Figure 3, in which a lower score reflects poorer pre-illness
social adjustment. If this finding is sustained for the larger sample, it raises the
issue of whether emotional overinvolvement results from having to care for an
individual with a long-term history of limited psychosocial competence or
whether it in fact contributes to the development of a poor premorbid history.

Further, Miklowitz found that patients categorized as being either from
low- or high-EE family environments could not be discriminated in the form
or severity of their schizophrenic symptomatology on the Brief Psychiatric
Rating Scale (BPRS) (Overall and Gorham, 1962) at admission or shortly
following discharge. However, when the high-EE cases were subdivided, those
from environments designated as high-EE solely on the basis of emotional
overinvolvement were significantly more symptomatic at discharge than those

Figure 2. Number of Intrusive Statements Expressed in Direct
Interaction by Mothers in Different EE Subgroups

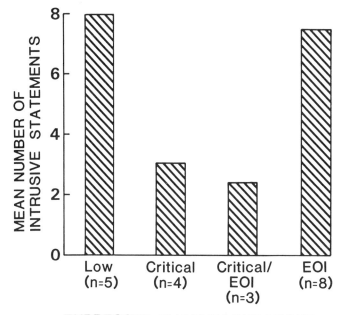

TOTAL NUMBER OF INTRUSIVE STATEMENTS
EXPRESSED IN DIRECT INTERACTION
BY MOTHERS IN DIFFERENT
EE SUBGROUPS

coming from high-EE environments defined by excess criticism (see Figure 4).
Thus, in this area, as well as in the study on affective style previously mentioned,
the strategy of breaking down the high-EE construct into substyles has proved
fruitful, while the dichotomous grouping of low- versus high-EE does not
always reveal major differences.

EE and Other Parent Characteristics. A fourth area of interest to family
researchers in schizophrenia concerns the relationship of EE to other parental
attributes shown in previous research to be associated with families of schizophrenics. As mentioned above, parental communication deviance has been
shown in a number of studies to be associated with offspring diagnosed as
schizophrenic (Wynne and others, 1976; Jones, 1977; Singer, 1967; Wild and
others, 1965, 1975). In the prospective study cited earlier, Doane and others
(1981) found that both communication deviance and a measure similar to EE
were independently predictive of the subsequent onset of schizophrenia-
spectrum disorders in disturbed adolescents. This finding suggests that adding

58

Figure 3. Relationship Between Premorbid Adjustment Scores
in the UCLA Social Attainment Scale and Parental EE Subgroups

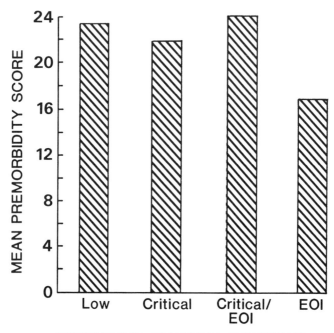

EE and PREMORBID STATUS

EXPRESSED EMOTION SUBGROUP

a measure of communication deviance to the EE variable might prove the prediction of relapse in already diagnosed schizophrenics. Currently, several
studies are underway that will examine this issue (Falloon and others, 1981;
Vaughn and others, 1982).

   Cross-Cultural Validity of EE. Another important issue concerning the
family's role in the course of schizophrenia is the question of whether findings
employing measures such as EE or CD are equally valid for cultural or subcultural groups other than the British and American cohorts studied to date.

   In a study in progress at the University of California, Los Angeles,
Karno (1981) is attempting to replicate the findings on EE and relapse rate in
a sample of Spanish-speaking Mexican-American families of schizophrenics.
He has found that the CFI, administered in the household setting, is well
accepted and responded to by the population. Preliminary trends from a pilot
study of nineteen families suggest a very striking difference in the incidence of
low-EE relatives in this population from that observed in the studies carried
out with Anglo populations. Of the nineteen cases whose relatives were
administered the CFI in this pilot study, only four (or 21 percent of the fam-

Figure 4. BPRS Scores Following Discharge
and Parental EE Subgroups

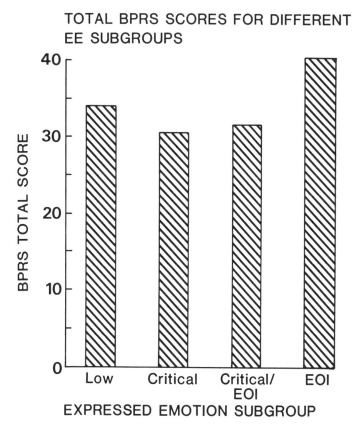

TOTAL BPRS SCORES FOR DIFFERENT
EE SUBGROUPS

ilies) were categorized as high-EE on the basis of Vaughn and Leff's criteria
(1976). This is in sharp contrast to the prevalence rate of approximately 67
percent in the studies by Vaughn and others and by Falloon mentioned
earlier. If this finding persists for the larger sample, it raises the important
issue of whether the criteria used for defining high-EE in English-speaking
cultures is appropriate for use in other cultural groups. Low rate of high-EE in
other culture groups might suggest that Anglo-American criteria used for
rating high-EE need to be recalibrated for other culture settings. Alternatively, a
lower prevalence rate of high-EE cases may be reflective of different familial
tolerance levels and response patterns to psychopathology, which might in
turn be associated with lower relapse rates.

Preliminary findings from the World Health Organization collaborative group studying EE and relapse in Chandigar, India, also indicate a low
incidence of high-EE relatives compared to those found in British and American samples (Day, 1982). These two pilot reports suggest that the EE con-

60

struct is complex and perhaps best understood in the context of the socio-ecological parameters of the culture in which it is measured.

Conclusion

The data reviewed in this paper indicate that recent research on the role of the family in schizophrenia is characterized by a closer attention to methodology and to a more precise specification of the family paramenters investigated. There appears to be a reasonable congruence between those variables found before the onset of a schizophrenic episode and those which relate to the subsequent course of the disorder once it appears. The strongest evidence for continuity from the pre-psychotic to the post-psychotic family environment is the affective climate of the family as reflected in the interview measure of EE or the interactional coding of AS. Families in which significant others, usually parents, express strongly critical or emotionally overinvolved attitudes are at higher risk for onset of and relapse for schizophrenia in offspring. The data from the prospective sample indicates that these affective attitudes predict schizophrenia only when associated with high levels of communication deviance. Thus, affective style appears to be a potentiator of life course from a disturbed adolescence to early adult schizophrenia or schizophrenia-like disorder. It does not appear to be uniquely linked to a life course directed towards schizophrenia, as numerous other outcomes can be noted when a negative affective style is associated with low levels of parental communication deviance.

The data with regard to the course of schizophrenia also reveal the significant role of parental affective evaluations in predicting relapse. It is not clear how a family attribute such as communication deviance, which is so significant for predicting onset, relates to relapse. If communication deviance is a necessary family property for the onset of schizophrenia, then it should bear a limited relationship to course as all families should manifest the attribute. On the other hand, there are different styles of communication deviance and variation in quantity even in those families designated as high-CD. Possibly, form and quantitative level of CD can provide additional information about the family environment of the newly released schizophrenic patient that can further understanding of how some environments foster recovery and others potentiate relapse.

References

Brown, G. W., Birley, J. L. T., and Wing, J. F. "Influence of Family Life on the Course of Schizophrenic Disorders: A Replication." *British Journal of Psychiatry,* 1972, *121,* 241–258.
Day, R. "Research on the Course and Outcome of Schizophrenia in Traditional Cultures: Some Potential Implications for Psychiatry in the Developed Countries." In M. J. Goldstein (Ed.), *Prevention Interventions in Schizophrenia: Are We Ready?* Washington, D.C.: U.S. Government Printing Office, 1982.

Doane, J. A., West, K. L., Goldstein, M. J., Rodnick, E. H., and James, J. E. "Parental Communication Deviance and Effective Style: Predictors of Subsequent Schizophrenic Spectrum Disorders in Vulnerable Adolescents." *Archives of General Psychiatry*, 1981, *38*, 679–685.

Falloon, I. R. H., Boyd, J. L., McGill, C. W., Strang, J. S., and Moss, H. B. "Family Management Training in the Community Care of Schizophrenia." In M. J. Goldstein (Ed.), *New Developments in Interventions with Families of Schizophrenics*. Vol. 12. San Francisco: Jossey-Bass, 1981.

Garmezy, N. "Children at Risk: The Search for the Antecedents of Schizophrenia. Part II: Ongoing Research Programs, Issues and Interventions." *Schizophrenia Bulletin*, 1974, *9*, 55–125.

Goldstein, M. J. "Further Data Concerning the Relation Between Premorbid Adjustment and Paranoid Symptomatology." *Schizophrenia Bulletin*, 1978, *4*, 236–243.

Goldstein, M. J., Rodnick, E. H., Jones, J. E., McPherson, S. R., and West, K. L. "Familial Precursors of Schizophrenia-Spectrum Disorders." In L. C. Wynne, R. L. Cromwell, and S. Matthysse (Eds.), *The Nature of Schizophrenia*, New York: Wiley, 1978.

Jones, J. E. "Patterns of Transactional Style Deviance in the TATs of Parents of Schizophrenics." *Family Process*, 1977, *16*, 327–337.

Jones, J. E., Wynne, L. C., Al-Khayyal, M., Doane, J. A., Ritzler, B., Singer, M. T., and Fisher, L. "Predicting Current School Competence of High-Risk Children with a Cross-Situational Measure of Parental Communication Deviance." In N. Watt, J. Anthony, L. C. Wynne, and J. Rolf (Eds.), *Children at Risk for Schizophrenia*. New York: Cambridge University Press, in press.

Karno, J. Personal communication, 1981.

Leff, J. P. "Schizophrenia and Sensitivity to the Family Environment." *Schizophrenia Bulletin*, 1976, *2*, 566–574.

Lewis, J. M. "Disorder Index of Risk for Schizophrenia." Doctoral dissertation, University of California, Los Angeles, 1979.

Lewis, J. M., Rodnick, E. H., and Goldstein, M. J. "Intrafamilial Interactive Behavior, Parental Communication Deviance, and Risk for Schizophrenia." *Journal of Abnormal Psychology*, 1981, *49* (5), 448–457.

Lidz, T., Fleck, S., and Corneilson, A. *Schizophrenia and the Family*. New York: International University Press, 1965.

Lieber, D. J. "Parental Focus of Attention in a Videotape Feedback Task as a Function of Hypothesized Risk for Offspring Schizophrenia." *Family Process*, 1977, *16*, 467–475.

Miklowitz, D. J. *Familial and Symptomatic Characteristics of Schizophrenics Living in High- and Low-EE Home Environments*. Unpublished master's thesis, University of California, Los Angeles, 1981.

Overall, J. E., and Gorham, D. R. "The Brief Psychiatric Rating Scale." *Psychological Reports*, 1962, *10*, 799.

Singer, M. "Family Transactions and Schizophrenia: 1. Recent Research Findings." In J. Romano (Ed.), *The Origins of Schizophrenia: Proceedings of the First Rochester International Conference in Schizophrenia*. Amsterdam: Excerpta Medica, 1967.

Strodtbeck, F. L. "The Family as a Three-Person Group." *American Sociological Review*, 1954, *19*, 23–29.

Sturgeon, D., Kuiper, L., Berkowitz, R., Turpin, G., and Leff, J. P. "Psychophysiological Responses of Schizophrenic Patients to High and Low Expressed Emotion Relatives." *British Journal of Psychiatry*, 1981, *138*, 46–50.

Tarrier, N., Vaughn, C., Lader, M., and Leff, J. P. "Bodily Reaction to People and Events in Schizophrenics." *Archives of General Psychiatry*, 1979, *36*, 311–315.

Vaughn, C. E., and Leff, J. P. "The Influence of Family and Social Factors on the Course of Psychiatric Illness: A Comparison of Schizophrenic and Depressed Neurotic Patients." *British Journal of Psychiatry*, 1976, *129*, 125–137.

Vaughn, C. E., Snyder, K. S., Freeman, W., Jones, S., Falloon, I. R. H., and Liberman, R. P. "Family Factors in Schizophrenic Relapse: A Replication." *Schizophrenia Bulletin*, 1982, *8*, 425–426.

Wender, P. H., Rosenthal, D., and Kety, S. S. "Psychiatric Assessment of the Adoptive Parents of Schizophrenics." In D. Rosenthal and S. S. Kety (Eds.), *The Transmission of Schizophrenia*. New York: Pergamon Press, 1968.

Wild, C., Shapiro, L., and Goldberg, L. "Transactional Communication Disturbances in Families of Male Schizophrenics." *Family Process*, 1975, *14*, 131–160.

Wild, C., Singer, M., Rosman, B., Ricci, J., and Lidz, T. "Measuring Disordered Styles of Thinking Using the Object Sorting Test on Parents of Schizophrenic patients." *Archives of General Psychiatry*, 1965, *13*, 471–476.

Wynne, L., Singer, M., Bartko, J., and Toohey, M. L. "Schizophrenics and Their Families: Recent Research on Parental Communication, in Psychiatric Research." In J. M. Tanner (Ed.), *Developments in Psychiatric Research: The Widening Perspective*. New York: International Universities Press, 1976.

Michael J. Goldstein in professor of clinical psychology at the University of California, Los Angeles. He has been a principal investigator for over twenty years on a comprehensive research program concerning family factors associated with the onset, course and treatment of major mental disorders, particularly schizophrenia. He recently has been selected to head one of the nodes of the MacArthur Foundation Network on Risk and Protective Factors in the Major Mental Disorders.

PART 2.

The Effects of
an Atypical Child
on Family Functioning

Problem children constitute a major source of stress and
disturbance for their families, although it is by no means apparent
that specific types of childhood disorders are associated with
specific family disturbances.

Families with Problem Children

Eric J. Mash

Problem children constitute a source of stress for the family (Hetherington and Martin, 1979). In fact, children do not have to be problem children to be stressful. They just have to be children. Infants and young children may produce the highest density of aversive events associated with any role in our culture (Patterson, 1982). Research suggests that the birth of a child frequently has adverse effects on the emotional status and attitudes of both parents (Blood and Wolfe, 1960; Hobbs and Cole, 1976), the marital relationship (Waldron and Routh, 1981), and the behavior of unsuspecting siblings (Dunn and Kendrick, 1980).

In most cases, parents are able to cope with the average expectable stresses created by their children. However, when a child is perceived as atypical or difficult, the mismatch between child and parent behavior is high and the amount of parenting-related stress increases dramatically (Bell and Harper, 1977). Even in nonclinical populations the birth of a child who is perceived to have major or persistent problems corrclates highy with parental reports of distress and negative affect (Weinburg and Richardson, 1981).

It is not surprising, therefore, that parents of identified problem children also report high levels of stress related to parenting. In our own research,

The work described in this chapter was supported by grants from Health and Welfare Canada, the Alberta Mental Health Research Council, and a Killam Resident Fellowship. The help of Charlotte Johnston and Sally During with the preparation of this chapter is gratefully acknowledged.

A. Doyle, D. Gold, D. S. Moskowitz (Eds.). *Children in Families Under Stress.*
New Directions for Child Development, no. 24. San Francisco: Jossey-Bass, June 1984.

we have found that mothers of hyperactive-aggressive, developmentally delayed, and abused children all report high levels of stress when compared with mothers of non-problem children. However, the types of stress reported are related to the nature of the child's problem and age. For example, although mothers of both developmentally delayed and hyperactive children reported high levels of stress related to child difficulty, only mothers of hyperactive children reported feeling socially isolated, depressed, and self-blaming (Mash and Johnston, 1983a, b). Such reports were especially evident for mothers of preschool-age hyperactive children. There is a need to consider the relationships between child problems and family dysfunction with respect to both the nature of the child's difficulty and the developmental status of both child and family.

For the widest possible range of childhood disorders one does not have to look too far or too long to identify related family disturbances. Relationships between family functioning and such diverse child problems as hyperactivity (Stewart and others, 1980), antisocial and delinquent behavior (Alexander, 1973; Patterson, 1982), neurotic and anxiety reactions (Britton, 1969), autism (Cantwell and others, 1979), psychosomatic disorders (Garner and Wenar, 1959), learning disabilities (Chapman and Boersma, 1979), retardation and developmental delay (Buckhalt and others, 1978; Waisbren, 1980), depression (Cantwell, 1983), abuse (Mash and others, in press), and neglect (Aragona and Eyberg, 1981) have all been demonstrated.

However, it is not clear at this stage of our research that specific childhood disorders are associated with specific types of family disturbance. Characteristic disturbances in family functioning for most problem child populations include marital conflict (O'Leary and Emery, 1983), disruptions in parent-child social interaction (Patterson, 1982), parental mood disturbances, especially depression (Griest and others, 1980; Patterson, 1980), disturbed sibling relationships (Brody and Stoneman, in press; Mash and Johnston, 1983c), and problems with social support systems (Wahler, 1981). The cumulative weight of these and other studies leaves little doubt of the strong associations between child and family disturbance. However, there is still much controversy surrounding the nature of these relationships and how they are to be assessed and interpreted.

The purpose of this chapter is to highlight several conceptual and methodological issues surrounding the study of functioning in families with problem children. The focus will be on the impact of the problem child on the family. However, this focus is necessarily one of convenience, since unidirectional models of influence are woefully inadequate for the description of social interactive process.

Conceptual Issues

Direction of Causality. An observed association between a child problem and some family characteristic may be interpreted in several ways. Both may be related to common constitutional factors. Alternatively, a family characteristic may be viewed successively as a primary etiological factor underlying the child's problem, a compensatory reaction to some innate child characteristic, a secondary reaction to the child's problem that was produced by some earlier mode of family functioning, or a factor that produces the disorder by interacting with some innate characteristic and continues to exacerbate the problem once it has developed (Bell, 1964). For a variety of reasons (Bell, 1968; Bell and Harper, 1977), the interpretation that family functioning represents the primary etiological factor in producng children's problems dominated work in the field. Almost two decades ago, in reaction this one-sided point of view, Bell (1964, 1968) cautioned against simplistic interpretations of the direction of causality in child-family relationships. In a thorough review of the parent–child interaction research from 1960 to 1970, Walters and Stinnett (1971) concluded that "the era of viewing children as solely products of their parents' influence is past, for it is recognized that children themselves exert powerful influences upon the parent–child relationship" (p. 100–101).

Although unidirectional approaches to the study of family relationships were likened to the understanding gained by having six blind men touching different parts of the same elephant, it is not clear that a thorough consideration of the elephant's reaction to being touched has done much to improve the situation. In spite of optimistic beginnings, it has become apparent that our ability to conceptualize reciprocal causal relationships has far exceeded our methods for studying them, although admittedly we are getting better at it (Cairns, 1979; Suomi and others, 1979). If our understanding of the processes underlying the relationships between childhood disturbance and family functioning is to progress, we will need to increase our efforts to design studies that include sequential data and utilize procedures that have recently been suggested for the analysis of such sequences (Allison and Liker, 1982; Cairns, 1979; Gottman and Ringland, 1981).

Additionally, it will be important to examine directionality of effect as a dynamic and relative concept that changes over time and with the situation. Although maternal behavior may be predicted by infant behavior during the first year of life, during the second year maternal behavior may be a more powerful predictor of infant response. The degree of influence of particular family members will also vary with the situational context, yet few studies have examined the directionality of influence in disturbed families as a function of situational factors.

Family Systems Emphasis. Basic to an understanding of families with problem children is how family functioning is conceptualized. In our own work, when we initially developed an observational coding system for studying disturbed familes, the *Response-Class Matrix,* (Mash and others, 1973), the two major headings that designated who was to be observed were "child" and "m(other)." This view of the family as consisting of "mothers and others" was not atypical of research with families. However, experience has told us that the conceptual, design, and measurement problems associated with the study of only mother–child dyadic social interchange are formidable, and, although there is an obvious need for the development of more complex models to describe family functioning, it is not without some trepidation that we accept this challenge.

Contemporary formulations of disturbed family functioning emanate primarily from the writings and empirical work of social learning theorists such as Patterson (1982) and Wahler (Wahler, 1980; Wahler and Dumas, in press); developmental psychologists such as Lewis (1982), Lamb (1977), Bell (Bell and Harper, 1977), Parke (1978), and Cochran and Brassard (1979); and the conceptualizations of family therapists such as Haley (1976), Minuchin (1974), Epstein (Epstein and others, 1982), and others (see Gurman and Kniskern, 1981). For the most part, these systems approaches conceptualize the family as an interactive unit, composed of individuals and subsystems, each possessing distinctive attributes, all of which interact with one another. Although it is apparent that such a conceptualization captures the richness and complexity that we see in families, there is also little doubt that our ability to conceptualize system complexity currently exceeds the measurement operations and research strategies we possess for studying it. For example, few psychometrically sophisticated instruments for assessing whole family variables are currently available. Even the more complex observational systems for studying family interactions (Reid, 1978) have cast their data in the form of dyadic interchanges. Better measures for assessing disturbed family functioning are sorely needed.

Studying Disturbed Families

General Approaches. Two general strategies have characterized the study of families with problem children. The first is reflected in those studies that have attempted to isolate the impact of problem children on families by manipulating circumscribed child behaviors under contrived laboratory circumstances to observe how adults react. The second has involved the identification of existing groups of problem children to contrast their family characteristics and interaction patterns with those observed in comparable groups of normal or disturbed children.

Child Effects Research. The laboratory studies of child effects have demonstrated clear relationships between a variety of common and "difficult" child behaviors and adult reactions. Child behaviors such as inattention and distractability (Chapman, 1979), uncontrollability (Bugental and others, 1980), defiance (Parke and Sawin, 1977), impatience (Matthews, 1977), low person orientation (Keller and Bell, 1979), unresponsiveness (Cantor and Gelfand, 1977), anger and negativity (Teyber and others, 1977), task failure (Mulhern and Passman, 1979), failure to imitate (Bates, 1975), and nonverbal unresponsiveness (Bates, 1976) have been shown to engender a variety of seemingly adverse adult reactions. These include the use of power-assertive, negative, and controlling disciplinary tactics; unassertive and weak communication styles; ridicule and interrogation; and frequent use of punishment.

The laboratory investigations have also demonstrated a number of other important points with relevance for the functioning of families with problem children. First, unlike most studies of disturbed children, which have a distinctively pathological focus, laboratory studies have typically provided us with the opportunity to observe adult reactions to the prosocial counterparts of the "difficult" child behaviors being studied. Where negative child behaviors have been shown to engender negative adult reactions, prosocial child behaviors such as smiling and attentiveness, responsiveness, high person orientation, willingness to make reparation for misdeeds, calmness, controllability, and success lead to adult reactions that include the use of rewards, praise and attention, inductive disciplinary styles, positive verbal and nonverbal communications, and the frequent use of feedback. These findings suggest that the long-term cumulative impact of problem children on family functioning may not solely be based on what they do, but also on what they do not do. From a preventive standpoint, we must be cognizant that the things that *do not* happen in disturbed families are a source of stress and are potentially as damaging as those things that do happen. In this regard, it is essential that we study normal family processess to identify and better understand the nature of the deficits that characterize disturbed families (Walsh, 1982).

Laboratory investigations also demonstrate the reciprocities that frequently characterize social interaction in disturbed families. That is, negative responses lead to negative ones, and positive responses to positive one. There is evidence to suggest that some of the interactional difficulties in disturbed families may reflect a failure to respond reciprocally to the prosocial behavior of other family members (Patterson, 1982; Rausch, 1965). For example, mothers of hyperactive children react less favorably, even when their child initiates appropriate interaction (Cunningham and Barkley, 1979; Mash and Johnston, 1982). This may well reflect the fact that positive behaviors occurring in the context of a negative relationship may not be perceived as positive. There is a need to further examine such contrast effects in social interaction sequences.

Laboratory studies have also demonstrated the importance of child, adult, and setting characteristics in moderating how different adults react to the same child behavior (Bates and Pettit, 1981). Chapman (1979) reported that, although mothers generally responded to inattentive and distractable behavior in their children in a controlling fashion, they used more control with younger than older children and with boys than girls. Bugental and others, (1980) reported that adults used less assertiveness and weaker forms of communication in response to uncontrollable child behavior, but only when the adult's perception of their power to control the child was less. The degree of situational structure has also been shown to influence adult reactions to child behavior (Bates, 1976).

Laboratory studies have also shown that child effects on adults involve both response-eliciting and response-shaping functions. Not only do negative child behaviors lead to more punitive adult reactions (Teyber and others, 1977), but the punitive reactions of adults are strengthened when followed by desired child behavior outcomes (Mulhern and Passman, 1979). In addition, laboratory studies have demonstrated that different adult reactions may be elicited simply on the basis of experimentally induced differential expectations about the same child (Stevens-Long, 1973). Finally, these studies have also demonstrated the "spread of effect" associated with encountering problematic child behavior. Not only do adults behave differently in response to "difficult" child behavior, they have also been shown to view the child who is the source of this behavior as less competent, less intelligent (Bates, 1976), and less likeable (Cantor and others, 1977).

In summary, child-effects laboratory studies show us how negative child behavior leads to negative and controlling adult behavior and, more generally, to less favorable attitudes and expectations about the child; provide us with ample evidence for the important role that moderator variables play in influencing adult reactions to child disturbances; and highlight the point that child behavior both elicits and shapes adult behavior. Finally, they alert us that family reactions to problem children are both direct responses to child behavior and indirect reactions based on the adult's preexisting expectations and values.

Disturbed–Normal Comparisons. A second strategy for describing the functioning of families with disturbed children has involved comparisons of interaction patterns in disturbed versus nondisturbed families. Earlier studies focused on interactions observed during contrived laboratory tasks such as the Revealed Differences Task (Strodtbeck, 1951), while more recent studies have observed interaction in the home or in laboratory analogues of naturalistic settings (Hughes and Haynes, 1978).

Most major reviews of this voluminous literature (Frank, 1965; Hetherington and Martin, 1979; Jacob, 1983; Walters and Stinnett, 1971) have concluded that numerous methodological problems associated with these studies make it difficult to identify consistent evidence of family influences on child pyschopathology or intrafamilial dimensions that distinguish normal from disturbed families. However, other reviewers, (Doane, 1978) have concluded that consistent interactional differences exist between normal and disturbed families in relation to such dimensions as family conflict and coalitions, flexibility versus rigidity, family effectiveness and efficiency, and styles of communication.

Assessment Issues. Given the general inadequacies of classification systems for describing childhood disorders (Achenbach, 1978), and an even greater lack of assessment devices and classification schemes for describing family functioning, it is not surprising that many of the findings related to functioning in families with problem children are inconclusive. The issue of adequate diagnoses has received much recent discussion, highlighting the need for more objective definitions of problem children. Recent attempts to develop Research Diagnostic Criteria appear promising in this regard (Loney, 1982; Spitzer and others, 1978), as do developments in the area of behavioral assessment (Mash and Terdal, 1981; Phillips and Ray, 1980). In addition, multivariate approaches, exemplified by the work of Loney and her colleagues (Loney and others, 1978) and Achenbach (Achenbach and Edelbrock, 1978, 1981), offer promise for the identification of subgroups of children whose family interactions might then be studied more closely. For example, Loney's work suggests that hyperactivity and aggression can be identified as independent dimensions and that measures of family functioning obtained from parental reports are more likely to be correlated with the aggression than the hyperactivity factor. If so, one might predict that the observed patterns of family interaction in the two subgroups of hyperactive children would also differ.

In spite of their complexity, problems associated with the assessment of childhood disorders seem minor when compared with those accompanying the assessment of family functioning. If we are to adopt a systems conceptualization, one approach might be to assess the whole family. Some researchers have taken this literally to mean that all family members must be present during observations. Although such interactions might be revealing, there is no reason to believe that they would be more revealing than the observation of other relevant family subsystems, such as the child alone and mother–child, father–child, or sibling interactions. Whether a particular subsystem is relevant will depend on a variety of factors, including the purposes of the assessment, the age and sex of the problem child, specific parental characteristics (that is, marital status, employment status, and level of education), and family demographics (that is, the number of children and frequency of their birth, and living arrangements). Although developmental psychologists are becoming more aware of the ecology of family subsystems, there is a need for basic normative information concerning how much time family members actually spend with one another, in what subgroups, and in what situations during different periods in the development of both the child and family. It is likely that the developmental processes being served by various family subsystems change over time, and various subsystems may fluctuate in their relative importance.

After much debate concerning whether family functioning should be assessed utilizing detailed interviews, questionnaires, rating scales, or direct observations of family interaction, current writers on this topic have stressed the need for multimethod assessments. There are, however, a few points concerning this issue that need to be addressed. The first concerns the notion that direct observation represents a more veridical measure than verbal report. Often when the correlation between verbal report and observation is low, the assumption is made that verbal report is inaccurate, presumably because it is more easily subject to bias and distortion. However, in light of what we know regarding family members' ability to regulate their behavior while being observed (Johnson and Lobitz, 1974), observational information can be easily distorted. Direct observations of family behavior are important but they tap only one dimension of family functioning, that is, behavioral interaction.

Verbal reports are appropriate for the assessment of perceptions and attitudes, not behavior, and when they are used as behavioral measures they can be most misleading. For example, there are numerous reports in the hyperactivity literature that present scores on parent-completed checklists as measures of "child behavior in the home." These checklist measures are indicative of parental perceptions and may or may not correspond to observed behavior. In utilizing verbal report measures in our own research, we have found that abusive mothers rate their preschool-age children as very problematic and at levels comparable to ratings by mothers of hyperactive children (Mash and others, in press). However, checklist ratings were not correlated with observed child behavior, in the case of abusive mothers, although they were with mothers of hyperactive children. In this instance, one might conclude that the verbal reports of abusive mothers were inaccurate, and this might be true in relation to child behavior. However, they may be highly accurate measures of parental perceptions of their children, and to the extent that these perceptions are also correlated with how abusive mothers interact with their children, they reflect an important dimension of family functioning. If we are to understand the contributions of parental attitudes in disturbed family interaction, and especially if we are to understand these attitudes as they occur in sequence with child behavior, it is essential that we develop better measures of parental perceptions and expectations that describe the internal rules governing parental behavior in specific situations.

A related issue is that of discrepant reports from different family members. When the reports by fathers differ from those of mothers, we sometimes assume that one informant in inaccurate, usually the father. However, it is apparent that such disagreement may be an accurate reflection of differing parental perceptions, and this in turn may have enormous significance. For example, Block and others (1981) reported that an objective index of parental agreement about childrearing issues and values at age three was, for boys, related to the quality of the child's psychological functioning several years later. This measure of agreement also predicted the continuation or termination of the marriage. Other studies point to the importance of considering parental perceptions even when they do not correspond to concomitantly observed child behavior. For example, Lee and Bates (1982) found that maternal perceptions of their six-month-old infants as difficult were the best predictions of later problems, even though they were not highly correlated with concomitant measures of infant behavior.

Another assessment issue concerns where observations of disturbed families should be conducted. Several studies have compared home versus clinic observations, and, not surprisingly, these observations frequently differ.

Often these discrepancies are taken to mean that clinic samples of family inter-actions are less reliable than observations in the natural environment. However, in these cases natural is equated with physical location of the obser-ver rather than with the functional properties of setting events for family behavior (Wahler and Fox, 1981). Meaningful samples of disturbed family functioning are those that tap representative contexts, and often such con-texts may be created or observed independently of physical location. There-fore, when conceptualized in this manner, observation in the clinic or play-room may be more naturalistic than observation in the home and may be a much more efficient way of sampling and summarizing family behaviors of interest. Alternatively, there may be times when home observations are more naturalistic. For example, if we wished to describe family resources, organiza-tion, scheduling or routines, home observations may provide more accurate measures.

The question of which family behaviors are to be assessed is of para-mount importance. From a measurement standpoint, the most sophisticated assessments have been of the social interactions of family dyads and the marital relationship and the affective status, global attitudes, and perceptions of individual family members. However, although the measurement systems that have been employed may be psychometrically sophisticated, it is not clear that they describe relevant family variables. In this regard, the assessment schemes of family therapists, such as Minuchin (1974), Epstein and others (1978), and Olson and others (1979) that focus more on family structure and function than content (Alexander, 1973) provide important leads, but require further psychometric elaboration. Also, empirically derived taxonomies that describe the social environments or climates of disturbed families such as those presented by Moos (Moos and Moos, 1978) and others (Beavers, 1982; Deykin, 1972; Pless and Satterwhite, 1973) describe important dimensions of family functioning. Such taxonomies of family disturbance, if combined with more specific assessments of social interaction, may help to elucidate the inter-play between the broader dimensions of family relationship and specific types of family interactions (Hinde, 1979).

A final point concerning assessment relates to possible differential reac-tive effects that specific methods may have on particular populations. Are some disturbed groups more likely to react to being observed than others? Anecdotally, in our own research it seemed that different groups reacted to observation in different ways. For example, four-to-nine-year-old hyperactive children seemed quite insensitive to the fact that we were observing them. In contrast, similar-age normal children appeared to be much more oriented to the observation mirrors, microphones, and being watched. We suspect that the nature of the hyperactive child's deficit may be implicated in their apparent unawareness of the general observational context (Douglas, 1980). Also, when we first started to observe abusive mothers we expected them to be defensive, on guard, and on their best behavior. Contrary to our expectations, abusive mothers appeared quite comfortable while being observed. It was our impression that the nonabusive mothers tended to react to the observational setting in a more socially conforming style than abusive mothers. That abusive mothers did not respond in a conforming manner is consistent with other observational studies (Reid and others, 1981) and questionnaire data (Egeland and others, 1979), and may reflect one dimension of their problem: a failure to regulate behavior in accordance with social demand characteristics. Possible interactions between methods of assessment and the population being studied should be considered when making comparisons across groups of disturbed families.

Selected Research Findings

In this section, I will describe some of our research experiences in studying families with problem children. Among the groups we have assessed are hyperactive-aggressive, developmentally delayed, and abused children, as well as comparison groups of normal children. Our general strategy has been to use standard methods to assess either individual family members or various family subsystems in each of the different populations. For the most part, we have obtained laboratory-playroom observations of mother–child interactions during a play and structured task situation. The specific findings from our research appear in a number of recent publications (Mash and Johnston, 1982; Mash and Johnston, 1983b,c,d; Mash and others, in press). Rather than present specific research findings in any detail here, I will highlight some of the processes that seemed to characterize the functioning of the disturbed families we have observed.

Many of the ideas to be presented are consistent with the systems models described by developmental psychologists such as Lewis (1982), Lamb (1977), and Parke (1978); in addition, there are Chapman's (1981) discussion of functional versus intentional control, Patterson's (1982) theory of reciprocity and coercion for socially aggressive families, Wahler's (Wahler and Dumas, in press) discussion of setting events and social networks, Bell's (Bell and Harper, 1977) notion of upper- and lower-limit controls, Hinde's (1979) distinction between interaction and relationship, Rausch's (1965) notions of control and organization, and Gottman and Ringland's (1981) discussion of dominance and bidirectionality. Many of these concepts describe similar processes. The discussion will be primarily in relation to dyadic social interchanges between mother and child, although it can easily be expanded to accommodate other family subsystems and their interrelationships.

Almost all the mothers we have observed interacting with their problem children appear to be, in Chapman's (1981) words, "set for trouble." This was true irrespective of the nature of the child's problem. Interview and checklist data indicated that all mothers perceived their children as either difficult, atypical, or unusual. Concomitant with this perception of difficulty was a perceived need to control their child. As previous research has shown, a parent's perception of their child as difficult may be influenced by child characteristics of a general (age or sex) or specific (interactional behavior) nature, and by parental characteristics that relate to role expectations, values, personality, or affective status. Whether the perception of child difficulty was accompanied by the perceived need to control the child's behavior appears to depend on the situational context. If a parent perceived the situation as requiring control—for example, when a task was to be completed, chores were to be done, visitors were in the home, or the family was shopping—then it was likely that controls would be used.

Since the perceived need to control the child reflects child characteristics, parental characteristics, and situational factors, mothers of children exhibiting different problems may all exercise high levels of control, but for very different reasons. This seems to fit with many of our observations of disturbed mother-child interactions. In structured situations requiring the child to complete several tasks in a brief time period, mothers of hyperactive, developmentally delayed, and abused children were all significantly more directive and controlling than mothers of normals. Such a response style seemed to occur regardless of the nature of the child's problem.

In our research (Mash and Johnston, 1982) and in other studies (Cunningham and Barkley, 1979) mothers of hyperactives have been shown to be extremely directive while interacting with their children in a structured task situation. That hyperactive children are also more negative and noncompliant in these circumstances suggests that maternal directiveness may be a reaction to disruptive and uncontrollable child behavior. Further support of an experimental nature comes from those studies (Barkley, 1981) reporting that mothers of hyperactive children become less controlling when their child is made more compliant through the use of stimulant medication.

For mothers of hyperactive children, the processes underlying their use of control seem to depend quite a bit on child characteristics. However, two findings should be noted. Sequential analyses of mother–child interaction indicate that a good deal of the mother's control does not occur immediately following the negative-noncompliant behavior of their children. In fact, mothers of hyperactive children are almost as likely to exercise control in response to child compliance as to child noncompliance. This pattern is consistent with findings reported by Chapman (1981), which he referred to as "anticipatory discipline" or "anticipatory control." Such discipline is viewed as involving intentional control, based on the mother's perceptions, plan, rules, or strategies and reflecting maternal behaviors that are primarily immediate reactions to child behavior during the interaction. The current findings suggest that the behavior of mothers of hyperactive children reflects both intentional and functional control but that the latter mode is probably dominant.

Is it the case that functional control of maternal behavior is the norm for mothers of hyperactive children? We explored this question (Mash and

Johnston, 1983b) by examining the extent to which we could predict the amount of control exercised by mothers with their hyperactive children, using two sets of predictor variables in a multiple-regression format. The first set involved child behaviors during the mother–child interaction; the second involved checklists reflecting the mothers' reports of self-esteem and stress behavior in the play and task situations. The only significant predictors of maternal control during play were child behaviors. However, mothers' use of control during the task situation was predicted by both child behavior and by mothers' reports of their self-esteem and stress. We presume that the unstructured play situation was viewed by mothers as not requiring control over their children; consequently, during play, the controls that were exerted represented reactions to what the child was doing, that is, primarily functional control. On the other hand, the task situation was perceived as requiring direction, and consequently intentional controls that reflected maternal self-perceptions appeared to be relevant as well.

Although we have not fully analyzed the data for our developmentally delayed and abusive samples, I would like to discuss some of our preliminary findings. Mothers of developmentally delayed children exercised high levels of control, not only during the task situation, but during the play situation as well (Mash and Johnston, 1983a). In fact, in terms of the number of directives issued to their children, play and task interactions were virtually indistinguishable. It is possible that the intentional control may reflect the adoption of a parental role of being a teacher for their developmentally delayed child. In any event, for mothers of developmentally delayed children, very little of their behavior appeared to be organized around the behavior of their child.

The pattern of control exercised by abusive mothers was similar to what we observed for hyperactive children. Abusive mothers were more controlling and directive, but primarily during the structured task situation. During play interactions their behavior was virtually indistinguishable from that of normal mothers, at least for the global behaviors described by our observational codes (Mash and others, in press).

While the pattern of controls exercised by the abusive mothers was similar to that for mothers of hyperactives, there was one very important difference. For all measures of child behavior we assessed for both play and task situations (for example, interaction, compliance, negative behavior, and questions), there were no observed differences between the abused children and the comparison group of normal children. While the behavior of hyperactive children had been extremely negative and noncompliant in the task situation, abused children were as compliant as normal children. Mothers of abused children exercised control during the task situation that did not appear to be functionally related to the behavior of their children. Abusive mothers exerted intentional control, organizing their behavior around expectations they had for their children and themselves, and were not interacting in a reciprocal or contingent fashion. These findings are consistent with those reported by

Egeland and others (1979) and Egeland and Brunnquell (1979) for a high-risk population of mothers. While there were few child characteristics that distinguished between groups of good and poor care, high-risk mothers, they could be distinguished on the basis of their perceptions concerning the psychological complexity of their child. In addition, Twentyman (Twentyman and others, 1982) reported findings supporting the view that abusive mothers may hold unrealistic expectations and attributions about childrens' behavior.

In general, our findings suggest that parents' perceptions regarding the need to control their problem children, and their subsequent use of controls, emanate from several sources. Such control may be a reflection of child characteristics and behavior and parental norms and expectations. Although the measurement tasks may be formidable, a conceptualization of parental perceptions of their disturbed children as part of a dynamic system of interaction rather than as static entities should have the greatest potential usefulness for understanding interactions in disturbed families. This view is consistent with the suggestions of others (Bell, 1979; Parke, 1978) that parental attitudes and cognitions need to be considered in sequence with child behavior.

In describing behaviors and perceptions in sequence it may be possible to identify different feedback systems for intentional versus functional forms of parental control. For example, child compliance and negative behavior may serve to punish parental attempts at control. However, at the same time, noncompliance and negative behavior may actually reinforce the parent's view that their child needs to be controlled. Consequently, parental beliefs regarding the need to control their child may be strengthened at the same time that their effectiveness to do so is diminished. This may explain why parents of problem children so often persist in their use of ineffective and unassertive forms of discipline in spite of their lack of effectiveness. At various points in the developmental sequence, the incongruence between the perceived need to control their child and an inability to do so may lead to heightening parental stress, increased depression, and lowered self-esteem in parents with disturbed children.

I will illustrate how such a dynamic developmental interplay might operate by examining some cross-sectional data we have collected with younger and older hyperactive children. Our data (Mash and Johnston, 1982) indicate that, although older (mean age = 8 years) hyperactive children are far less disruptive than their younger (mean age = 4 years) counterparts, maternal perceptions of their children as problematic do not appear to show age-related differences. Although the mother–child interactions for older hyperactive children were not very different from normal children, mothers continued to view their children as exhibiting levels of disturbance comparable to the younger hyperactive children. Although it is conceivable that our observation setting was insensitive to problems of older hyperactive, children, such as difficulties with peers, it is also possible that maternal perceptions of the child as difficult and in need of control have been reinforced and maintained somewhat independently of the child's current behavior. In fact, if the hyperactive child were to reduce gradually his level of negativity, it is possible that parental perceptions of child difficulty could actually be strengthened by being placed on an intermittent schedule. Each infrequently occurring incident of child noncompliance could serve to strengthen the parents' view of a difficult child.

Some other age-related findings with parents of hyperactive children also point to the potential importance of examining the sequential interplay between attitudes and behavior as they influence outcomes in families with problem children. As part of our assessment, we obtained parental reports of self-esteem related to parenting. Parents of hyperactive children reported less confidence in possessing the necessary skill and knowledge to be a good parent and reported finding less value and comfort in their parental role when contrasted with parents of normal children (Mash and Johnston, 1983c). However, in contrasting parents of younger and older hyperactive children, both mothers and fathers of older hyperactive children reported less confidence in having the knowledge and skill to be good parents, relative to parents of younger hyperactive children. The one item that best discriminated between the parents of younger and older hyperactive children was whether the mother believed she could help her child with a problem. Parents of older hyperactive children consistently answered in the negative. In contrast to these findings for self-reported skill and knowledge, the reports of parents of hyperactive children in regard to how much they valued their role as parents were lower than for normal children but comparable for the younger and older groups. It would appear that these types of normative values reflect broader and more stable sociocultural dimensions.

We also assessed the relationship between the extent to which parents perceived their children as difficult or problematic and their reported self-esteem as parents (Mash and Johnston, 1983c). These correlations were consistently negative. Parents who perceived their children as problematic reported lower levels of self-esteem. This was true for both mothers and fathers. Interestingly enough, fathers' perceptions of their children as difficult were correlated with mothers' reported self-esteem in relation to their possession of the skill and knowledge necessary to be a good parent; thus mothers' views concerning their own competence as parents may relate to how their husbands view the child. Mothers of problem children appeared to be more stressed when fathers viewed the child in a negative light. These preliminary data speak to the issues of subsystem relationships and interdependencies in families with problem children. It is evident from recent work that the fathers' relationship with both the child and mother may be extremely important in understanding the mother–child subsystem (Lewis and others, 1982).

The findings described in this section illustrate some of the ways that disturbed child behaviors interact with parental appraisals in specific situations to determine how mothers may control their problem child's behavior. More detailed interactional analyses for different populations of children are needed to assess adequately some of the suggestions that have been made. In addition, similar analyses of the problem child interacting with other family members are needed.

Summary

Research findings suggest a strong association between childhood behavior problems and disturbances in family functioning. Commonly identified family problems across families with a diverse range of problem children include marital conflict, disruptions in behavioral interactions and nonverbal and verbal communications, parental mood disturbance (especially depression), lowered self-esteem, disrupted sibling relationships, and problematic interactions with relatives, friends, and social service agencies. One cannot draw conclusions yet as to whether these disturbances reflect nonspecific reactions to the stresses associated with having a problem child or specific effects related to the unique characteristics of a particular childhood disorder. Research findings with populations of hyperactive, developmentally delayed, abused, and normal children suggest commonalities in the mother–child interaction patterns for all groups, particularly in relation to parents' use of controls. However, group differences also suggest that the processes underlying parental behaviors may differ across groups, reflecting multiple sources of influence involving child behaviors and characteristics, parental attitudes and perceptions, and situational context.

Although the association between child disturbance and family disturbance is strong, interpretations regarding directionality of influence are ambiguous. Although previous research has emphasized the etiological role of the family as an antecedent for child psychopathology, current findings related to the impact of newborn children on the family and laboratory studies that isolate child effects on adults strongly suggest many disturbed-child effects on the family. Recent work in the areas of developmental psychology and child psychopathology have adopted systems models involving reciprocal relationships between family subsystems. Such models require that the nature of mutual influences in different situations and at varying developmental stages for both child and family be described. Although current models of family systems and reciprocal influence have much potential, there are a number of measurement issues related to the assessment of family functioning that need to be addressed if this potential is to be realized.

References

Achenbach, T. M. "Psychopathology of Childhood: Research Problems and Issues." *Journal of Consulting and Clinical Psychology,* 1978, *46,* 759–776.
Achenbach, T. M., and Edelbrock, C. S. "The Classification of Child Psychopathology: A Review and Analysis of Empirical Efforts." *Psychological Bulletin,* 1978, *85,* 1275–1301.

Achenbach, T. M., and Edelbrock, C. S. "Behavioral Problems and Competencies Reported by Parents of Normal and Disturbed Children Aged Four Through Sixteen." *Monographs of the Society for Research in Child Development*, 1981, *46*, 1–82.

Alexander, J. F. "Defensive and Supportive Communications in Normal and Deviant Families." *Journal of Consulting and Clinical Psychology*, 1973, *40*, 223–231.

Allison, P. D., and Liker, J. K. "Analyzing Sequential Categorical Data on Dyadic Interaction: A Comment on Gottmann." *Psychological Bulletin*, 1982, *91*, 393–403.

Aragona, J. A., and Eyberg, S. M. "Neglected Children: Mothers' Report of Child Behavior Problems and Observed Verbal Behavior." *Child Development*, 1981, *52*, 596–602.

Barkley, R. A. "The Use of Psychopharmacology to Study Reciprocal Influences in Parent-Child Interaction." *Journal of Abnormal Child Psychology*, 1981, *9*, 303–310.

Bates, J. E. "Effects of a Child's Imitation Versus Nonimitation on Adult's Verbal and Nonverbal Positivity." *Journal of Personality and Social Psychology*, 1975, *31*, 840–851.

Bates, J. E. "Effects of Children's Nonverbal Behavior on Adults." *Child Development*, 1976, *47*, 1079–1088.

Bates, J. E., and Pettit, G. S. "Adult Individual Differences as Moderators of Child Effects." *Journal of Abnormal Child Psychology*, 1981, *9*, 329–340.

Beavers, W. R. "Healthy, Midrange, and Severely Dysfunctional Families." In F. Walsh (Ed.), *Normal Family Processes*. New York: The Guilford Press, 1982.

Bell, R. Q. "The Effects on the Family of a Limitation in Coping Ability in the Child: A Research Approach and Finding." *Merrill-Palmer Quarterly*, 1964, *10*, 129–142.

Bell, R. Q. "A Reinterpretation of the Direction of Effects in Studies of Socialization." *Psychological Review*, 1968, *75*, 81–95.

Bell, R. Q. "Parent, Child, and Reciprocal Influences." *American Psychologist*, 1979, *34*, 821–826.

Bell, R. Q., and Harper, L. V. *Child Effects on Adults*. Hillsdale, N.J.: Erlbaum, 1977.

Block, J. H., Block, J., and Morrison, A. "Parental Agreement-Disagreement on Childrearing Orientations and Gender-Related Personality Correlates in Children." *Child Development*, 1981, *52*, 965–974.

Blood, R. O., and Wolfe, D. M. *Husbands and Wives: The Dynamics of Married Living*. New York: Free Press, 1960.

Britton, R. S. "Psychiatric Disorders in the Mothers of Disturbed Children." *Journal of Child Psychology and Psychiatry*, 1969, *10*, 245–258.

Brody, G. H., and Stoneman, Z. "Children with Atypical Siblings: Socialization Outcomes and Clinical Participation." In B. Lahey and A. E. Kazdin (Eds.), *Advances in Clinical Child Psychology*. Vol. 5. New York: Plenum, 1983.

Buckhalt, J. A., Rutherford, R. B., and Goldberg, K. E. "Verbal and Nonverbal Interaction of Mothers with Their Down's Syndrome and Nonretarded Infants." *American Journal of Mental Deficiency*, 1978, *83*, 337–343.

Bugental, D. B., Caporeal, L., and Shennum, W. A. "Experimentally Produced Child Uncontrollability: Effects on the Potency of Adult Communication Patterns." *Child Development*, 1980, *51*, 520–528.

Cairns, R. B. (Ed.). *The Analysis of Social Interactions: Methods, Issues, and Illustrations*. Hillsdale, N.J.: Erlbaum, 1979.

Cantor, N. L., and Gelfand, D. M. "Effects of Responsiveness and Sex of Children on Adult Behavior." *Child Development*, 1977, *48*, 232–238.

Cantor, N. L., Wood, D. D., and Gelfand, D. M. "Effects of Responsiveness and Sex of Children on Adult Males' Behavior." *Child Development*, 1977, *48*, 1426–1430.

Cantwell, D. P. "Childhood Depression: A Review of Current Research." In B. Lahey and A. E. Kazdin (Eds.), *Advances in Clinical Child Psychology*. Vol. 5. New York: Plenum, 1983.

Cantwell, D. P., Baker, L., and Rutter, M. "Families of Autistic and Dysphasic Children. I. Family Life and Interaction Patterns." *Archives of General Psychiatry,* 1979, *36,* 682–687.

Chapman, M. "Listening to Reason: Children's Attentiveness and Parental Discipline." *Merrill-Palmer Quarterly,* 1979, *25,* 251–263.

Chapman, M. "Isolating Causal Effects Through Experimental Changes in Parent-Child Interaction." *Journal of Abnormal Child Psychology,* 1981, *9,* 321–327.

Chapman, J. W., and Boersma, F. J. "Learning Disabilities, Locus of Control, and Mother Attitudes." *Journal of Educational Psychology,* 1979, *71,* 250–258.

Cochran, M. M., and Brassard, J. A. "Child Development and Personal Social Networks." *Child Development,* 1979, *50,* 601–616.

Cunningham, C. E., and Barkley, R. A. "A Comparison of the Interactions of Hyperactive and Normal Children with Their Mothers in Free Play and Structured Task." *Child Development,* 1979, *50,* 217–224.

Deykin, E. "Life Functioning in Families of Delinquent Boys: An Assessment Model." *Social Service Review,* 1972, *46,* 90–102.

Doane, J. A. "Family Interaction and Communication Deviance in Disturbed and Normal Families: A Review of Research." *Family Process,* 1978, *17,* 357–376.

Douglas, V. I. "Higher Mental Processes in Hyperactive Children: Implications for Training." In R. M. Knights and D. J. Bakker (Eds.), *Treatment of Hyperactive and Learning Disordered Children: Current Research.* Baltimore, Md.: University Park Press, 1980.

Dunn, J., and Kendrick, C. "The Arrival of a Sibling: Changes in Interaction Between Mother and First-Born Child." *Journal of Child Psychology and Psychiatry,* 1980, *21,* 119–132.

Egeland, B., and Brunnquell, D. "An At-Risk Approach to the Study of Child Abuse: Some Preliminary Findings." *Journal of the American Academy of Child Psychiatry,* 1979, *18,* 219–235.

Egeland, B., Deinard, A. Brunnquell, D., Phipps-Yonas, S., and Crichton, L. *Final Report: A Prospective of the Antecedents of Child Abuse.* Unpublished manuscript, University of Minnesota, Minneapolis, 1979.

Epstein, N. B., Bishop, D. S., and Levin, S. "The McMaster Model of Family Functioning." *Journal of Marriage and Family Counseling,* 1978, *4,* 19–31.

Epstein, N. B., Bishop, D. S., and Baldwin, L. M. "McMaster Model of Family Functioning: A View of the Normal Family." In F. Walsh (Ed.), *Normal Family Processes.* New York: The Guilford Press, 1982.

Frank, G. H. "The Role of the Family in the Development of Psychopathology." *Psychological Bulletin,* 1965, *64,* 191–205.

Garner, A. M., and Wenar, G. *The Mother-Child Interaction in Psychosomatic Disorders.* Urbana: University of Illinois Press, 1959.

Gottman, J. M., and Ringland, J. T. "The Analysis of Dominance and Bidirectionality in Social Development." *Child Development,* 1981, *52,* 393–412.

Griest, D. L., Forehand, R., Wells, K. C., and McMahon, R. J. "An Examination of Differences Between Nonclinic and Behavior-Problem Clinic-Referred Children and Their Mothers." *Journal of Abnormal Psychology,* 1980, *89,* 497–500.

Gurman, A. S., and Kniskern, D. P. (Eds.). *Handbook of Family Therapy.* New York: Brunner/Mazel, 1981.

Haley, J. *Problem Solving Therapy.* San Francisco: Jossey-Bass, 1976.

Hetherington, E. M., and Martin, B. "Family Interaction." In H. C. Quay and J. S. Werry (Eds.), *Psychopathological Disorders of Childhood.* New York: Wiley, 1979.

Hinde, R. A. *Towards Understanding Relationships.* London: Academic Press, 1979.

Hobbs, D. F., and Cole, S. B. "Transition to Parenthood: A Decade of Replication." *Journal of Marriage and the Family,* 1976, *38,* 723–731.

Hughes, H. M., and Haynes, S. N. "Structured Laboratory Observation in the Behavioral Assessment of Parent-Child Interactions: A Methodological Critique." *Behavior Therapy,* 1978, *9,* 428–447.

Jacob, T. "Interaction in Disturbed and Normal Families." *Psychological Bulletin,* 1983, *82,* 33–65.

Johnson, S. M., and Lobitz, C. K. "The Personal and Marital Adjustment of Parents as Related to Observed Child Deviance and Parenting Behavior." *Journal of Abnormal Child Psychology,* 1974, *2,* 193–207.

Keller, B. B., and Bell, R. Q. "Child Effects on Adults' Method of Eliciting Altruistic Behavior." *Child Development,* 1979, *50,* 1004–1009.

Lamb, M. "A Re-examination of the Infant Social World." *Human Development,* 1977, *20,* 65–85.

Lee, C. L., and Bates, J. E. "Mother-Child Interaction Years and Perceived Difficult Temperament." Unpublished manuscript, Department of Psychology, University of Indiana, Bloomington, 1982.

Lewis, M. "The Social Network Systems Model: Toward a Theory of Social Development." In T. Field, A. Huston, H. Quay, L. Troll, and G. Finley (Eds.), *Review of Human Development.* New York: Wiley, 1982.

Lewis, M., Feiring, C., and Weinraut, M. "The Father as a Member of the Child's Social Network." In M. E. Lamb (Ed.), *The Role of the Father in Child Development.* (2nd ed.) New York: Wiley, 1982.

Loney, J. "Research Diagnostic Criteria for Childhood Hyperactivity." Paper presented at the annual meeting of the American Psychopathological Association, New York, 1982.

Loney, J., Langhouse, J., and Paternite, C. "An Empirical Basis for Subgrouping the Hyperkinetic/Minimal Brain Dysfunction Syndrome." *Journal of Abnormal Psychology,* 1978, *87,* 434–441.

Mash, E. J., and Terdal, L. G. (Eds.). *Behavioral Assessment of Childhood Disorders.* New York: The Guilford Press, 1981.

Mash, E. J., and Johnston, C. "A Comparison of the Mother-Child Interactions of Younger and Older Hyperactive and Normal Children." *Child Development,* 1982, *53,* 1371–1381.

Mash, E. J., and Johnston, C. "A Comparison of the Mother-Child Interactions of Developmentally Delayed and Normal Children During Play and Task Situations." Manuscript in preparation, University of Calgary, Calgary, Alberta, 1983a.

Mash, E. J., and Johnston, C. "Parental Perceptions of Child Behavior Problems, Parenting, Self-Esteem, and Mothers' Reported Stress in Younger and Older Hyperactive and Normal Children." *Journal of Consulting and Clinical Psychology,* 1983b, *51,* 86–99.

Mash, E. J., and Johnston, C. "Sibling Interactions of Hyperactive and Normal Children and Their Relationship to Reports of Maternal Stress and Self-Esteem." *Journal of Clinical Child Psychology,* 1983c, *12,* 91–99.

Mash, E. J., and Johnston, C. "A Note on the Prediction of Mothers' Behavior with Their Hyperactive Children During Play and Task Situations." *Child Behavior Therapy,* 1983d, in press.

Mash, E. J., Terdal, L. G., and Anderson, K. "The Response-Class Matrix: A Procedure for Recording Parent-Child Interactions." *Journal of Consulting and Clinical Psychology,* 1973, *40,* 163–164.

Mash, E. J., Johnston, C., and Kovitz, K. "A Comparison of the Mother-Child Interactions of Physically Abused and Nonabused Children During Play and Task Situations." *Journal of Clinical Child Psychology,* in press.

Matthews, K. A. "Caregiver-Child Characteristics in the Type A Coronary-Prone Behavior Pattern." *Child Development,* 1977, *48,* 1852–1856.

Minuchin, S. *Families and Family Therapy.* Cambridge, Mass.: Harvard University Press, 1974.

Moos, R. H., and Moos, B. S. "A Typology of Family Social Environments." *Family Process,* 1978, *17,* 357–371.

Mulhern, R. K., and Passman, R. H. "The Child's Behavioral Pattern as a Determinant of Maternal Punitiveness." *Child Development,* 1979, *50,* 815–820.

O'Leary, K. D., and Emery, R. E. "Marital Discord and Child Behavior Problems." In M. D. Levine and P. Satz (Eds.), *Developmental Variation and Dysfunction.* New York: Academic Press, 1983.

Olson, D. H., Sprenkle, D. H., and Russell, C. S. "Circumplex Model of Marital and Family Systems: Cohesion and Adaptability Dimensions, Family Types, and Clinical Application." *Family Process,* 1979, *18,* 3–28.

Parke, R. D. "Parent-Infant Interaction: Progress, Paradigms, and Problems." In G. P. Sackett (Ed.), *Observing Behavior,* Vol. I: *Theory and Applications in Mental Retardation.* Baltimore: University Park Press, 1978.

Parke, R. D., and Sawin, D. B. "The Child's Role in Sparing the Rod." Unpublished manuscript, University of Illinois, Champaign, 1977.

Patterson, G. R. "Mothers: The Unacknowledged Victims." *Monographs of the Society for Research in Child Development,* 1980, *45,* 1–64.

Patterson, G. R. *Coercive Family Process.* Eugene, Ore.: Castalia, 1982.

Phillips, J. S., and Ray, R. S. "Behavioral Approaches to Childhood Disorders." *Behavior Modification,* 1980, *4,* 3–24.

Pless, I. B., and Satterwhite, B. "A Measure of Family Functioning and Its Application." *Social Science and Medicine,* 1973, *7,* 613–621.

Rausch, H. L. "Interaction Sequences." *Journal of Personality and Social Psychology,* 1965, *2,* 487–499.

Reid, J. B. (Ed.). *A Social Learning Approach to Family Intervention.* Vol. 2. Eugene, Ore.: Castalia, 1978.

Reid, J. B., Taplin, P. S., and Leober, R. "A Social Interactional Approach to the Treatment of Abusive Families." In R. Stuart (Ed.), *Violent Behavior: Social Learning Approaches to Prediction, Management, and Treatment.* New York: Brunner/Mazel, 1981.

Spitzer, R. L., Endicott, J., and Robins, E. "Research Diagnostic Criteria: Rationale and Reliability." *Archives of General Psychiatry,* 1978, *35,* 773–782.

Stevens-Long, J. "The Effect of Behavioral Context on Some Aspects of Adults' Disciplinary Practice and Affect." *Child Development,* 1973, *44,* 476–484.

Stewart, M. A., DeBlois, C. S., and Cummings, C. "Psychiatric Disorder in the Parents of Hyperactive Boys and Those with Conduct Disorders." *Journal of Child Psychology and Psychiatry,* 1980, *21,* 283–292.

Strodtbeck, F. L. "Husband-Wife Interaction Over Revealed Differences." *American Sociological Review,* 1951, *16,* 468–473.

Suomi, S., Lamb, M., and Stephenson, G. (Eds.). *Social Interaction Analysis: Methodological Issues.* Madison: University of Wisconsin Press, 1979.

Teyber, E. C., Messe, L. A., and Stollak, G. E. "Adult Response to Child Communications." *Child Development,* 1977, *48,* 1577–1582.

Twentyman, C. T., Rohrbeck, C. A., and Amish, P. L. *A Cognitive-Behavioral Reformulation of the Role Reversal Process.* Rochester, N.Y.: University of Rochester, 1982.

Wahler, R. G. "The Insular Mother: Her Problems in Parent-Child Treatment." *Journal of Applied Behavior Analysis,* 1980, *134,* 207–219.

Wahler, R. G., and Dumas, J. E. "A Chip Off the Old Block: Some Interpersonal Characteristics of Coercive Children Across Generations." In P. Strain (Ed.), *Children's Social Behavior: Development, Assessment, and Modification.* New York: Academic Press, in press.

Wahler, R. G., and Fox, J. J. "Setting Events in Applied Behavior Analysis: Toward a Conceptual and Methodological Expansion." *Journal of Applied Behavior Analysis,* 1981, *14,* 327–338.

Waisbren, S. E. "Parents' Reactions After the Birth of a Developmentally Disabled Child." *American Journal of Mental Deficiency,* 1980, *84,* 345–351.

Waldron, H., and Routh, D. K. "The Effect of the First Child on the Marital Relationship." *Journal of Marriage and the Family,* 1981, *43,* 785–788.

Walsh, F. (Ed.). *Normal Family Processes.* New York: The Guilford Press, 1982.

Walters, J., and Stinnett, N. "Parent-Child Relationships: A Decade Review of Research." *Journal of Marriage and the Family,* 1971, *33,* 70–111.

Weinberg, S. L., and Richardson, M. S. "Dimensions of Stress in Early Parenting." *Journal of Consulting and Clinical Psychology,* 1981, *49,* 686–693.

Eric J. Mash is professor of psychology at the University of Calgary. He is coeditor of Behavioral Assessment of Child Disorders *(Guilford Press, 1981) and has served as an associate editor for* Behavioral Assessment *(Pergamon Press). His primary research interests are in the areas of family interaction, child psychopathology, and behavioral assessment.*

Illustrations of the bidirectional nature of parent–child interactions
are provided in families with developmentally delayed children.

Social Interactions:
A Transactional Approach with
Illustrations from Children
with Developmental Problems

Linda S. Siegel
Charles E. Cunningham

The purpose of this chapter is to outline some transactional research strategies in the study of parent, child, and peer interactions that illustrate the influences of parents and children on each other. Although parents influence development, children have a role in determining the behavior of their parents. In the study of stress in families, we believe that methods that capture the bidirectional nature of the interaction should be used.

The critical question is how to identify and study these mutually interacting influences. A number of conceptual and methodological difficulties with this approach have been discussed in detail by Mash (Chapter Four). In this chapter, we will discuss several specific research strategies for assessing the effects of two possible sources of stress within the parent–child relationship— prematurity and developmental delay—and how these might relate to patterns

The preparation of this chapter was supported by grants from the Ontario Mental Health Foundation and the March of Dimes Birth Defects Foundation.

A. Doyle, D. Gold, D. S. Moskowitz (Eds.). *Children in Families Under Stress.*
New Directions for Child Development, no. 24. San Francisco: Jossey-Bass, June 1984.

of parent–child interaction. In both these cases, the children may be perceived as different by the parents and may elicit parental behaviors that are to some extent atypical. Children with developmental difficulties provide a means of examining the relationship between child behavior and adult responsiveness to the child. If there are differential patterns of responsiveness in these groups, then at least one possibility is that children have a significant role as determinants of parents' behavior.

Prematurity and Parent–Child Interactions

The birth of a very low birthweight, pre-term child represents a significant and stressful event in the life of the family. The early birth is often unexpected and, in the case of a very small infant, typically necessitates an extended hospital stay and numerous medical interventions. The interaction of the parents with the child in the neonatal period is thus limited. The child must live in an oxygen-, temperature-, and humidity-controlled environment, often with mechanically administered feeding and respiration. The subsequent course of its interaction with others may be affected. Although relatively little is known about the influences of this atypical situation, a number of studies have found differences between the interactions of parents with their pre-term and with their full-term children in the early months (Goldberg, 1978). These differences may persist throughout the first two years (for example, Crawford, 1982; Field and others, 1981). However, it is important to note that Crawford (1982) found that mothers of pre-term infants treated their infants in a manner similar to younger full-term infants. That is, the behavior of the mothers of pre-term infants was generally equivalent to that of mothers whose full-term infants were of equivalent ages to the pre-terms if their ages were corrected for their degree of prematurity. The mothers appeared to match their behavior to the child's level of development rather than to the child's chronological age. We will describe other instances of such calibration later in this chapter.

Prematurity also provides us with a means of studying the effects of developmental delay on interactions since pre-term infants are more likely to be delayed (for example, Hunt, 1981, 1982; Siegel, 1982a; Siegel and others, 1982). It may be the presence of a delayed child rather than the effects of the early atypical environment that result in different parent–child interaction patterns.

In this study we used the HOME (Home Observation for Measurement of the Environment, for example, Bradley and Caldwell, 1976) scale as a measure of the children's environment and the type of stimulation and responsiveness provided by the parents. We were interested in determining whether the environments of pre-term and full-term children would differ significantly. The extent to which parents responded differentially to developmentally delayed children regardless of their condition was also examined. Would delayed children elicit different patterns of parental stimulation than non-delayed children? That is, have the parents of more competent children provided more stimulating environments or do the parents use more effective strategies because their children are more responsive? While such a comparison by itself cannot establish whether delayed children elicit different patterns of parental stimulation than do non-delayed children or whether the parents of more competent children have provided more stimulating environments, examination of environment and child status over time might be more enlightening about the causal sequence than studies involving observations made at only one point.

The children in this study were part of an ongoing longitudinal project that involved the assessment of very low birthweight (< 1501 grams) infants and a group of demographically matched controls. The pre-term and full-term children were matched on socioeconomic status, parity, and maternal age at the time of the child's birth. The children were administered the HOME scale at one, three, and five years of age, the Bayley Scales at one year, the Stanford-Binet at three years, and the McCarthy Scales of Children's Abilities at five years. Further details of this study are available in Siegel (1982 a, b, c; 1983).

The HOME scale measures several dimensions of the child's home environment and is based on a combination of direct observation and structured home interview. It includes questions such as "Mother responds to child's vocalizations with a verbal response," "Mother does not shout at child during visit," "Mother provides eye-hand coordination toys." The HOME scale allows a more detailed assessment of the environment than do measures of socioeconomic status but, obviously, not as extensive as direct observations of parent–child interaction. The HOME scale, however, is less expensive and easier to administer than most observational measures.

We expected that prematurity, the associated parent–child separation, and parental concern about the medical condition of the child would influence the course of parent–child interactions. There were no differences between the pre-term and full-term children on the HOME scale scores at any age. These findings were also found in another sample of pre-term and full-term children whose interaction and attachment patterns with parents at one year of age were directly observed (Shattuck and others, 1983). Rode and others (1981) also found that the attachment patterns of pre-term and seriously ill infants did not differ from the patterns found in normal children.

Since we are interested in the influence that delayed development might have on the type of environment provided by the parent, we compared the HOME scores of the children who were delayed at a particular point with those who were not delayed to determine whether there would be any measurable environmental differences as a function of developmental level. Delay was defined as a score of one or more standard deviations below the mean of a particular cognitive test. The pattern of results showed some clear differences in developmental trends. At one year, there were some significant differences in HOME scores between the delayed and normally functioning children. At three years there were many more differences between the delayed and non-

88

delayed children. At five years, the children who were delayed had lower HOME scores than those who were not delayed and, again, many more of these differences were significant. Therefore, the differences in HOME scores between the delayed and non-delayed children increase with increasing age. While it is by no means conclusive evidence, this type of pattern suggests that the environment of delayed and non-delayed children diverges over time. At three and five years, there were many differences, so parents who were not initially responding differentially to developmental delay were responding differently later on. The delayed child may be less responsive and may provide insufficient cues to the family for appropriate toys and activities. The influence of the delayed child is more pervasive as the child gets older.

A similar trend is apparent if one considers the correlations of concurrent mental functioning and the HOME scores. As can be seen in Table 1, there were no significant relationships between the environment and the mental test scores at one year. These earlier test scores may be a reflection of the child's developmental level relatively independent of environmental influences. The relationships between mental test scores and HOME scores are significant at three and five years. Although causality of direction cannot be inferred from these data, it is possible that early test scores are a reflection of the child's developmental level independent of environmental influences, while parents and children exercise greater influences on each other later in development.

Positive Feedback Loop. The increasing influence of the delayed child on parent behavior as the child ages suggests that a positive feedback loop is operating. The young delayed child fails to provide the appropriate cues for parent behavior, the parent responds with inadequate stimulation for development, the child becomes more delayed due to a non-optimal environment, and it becomes even harder for the parents to provide the appropriate environment.

Table 1. Correlations Between HOME Scores
and Concurrent Mental Tests

| | *Age in Years* | | |
	1 *Bayley MDI*	*3* *Stanford-Binet*	*5** *McCarthy GCI*
Full-term			
75–76	ns	.488**	.69**
77–78	ns	.54**	
Pre-term			
75–76	ns	ns	.422**
77–78	ns	.38***	

*The 77–78 cohort was not seen at 5 years.
**$p < .001$
***$p < .01$

As both Mash and Hetherington have noted in this sourcebook (Chapters One and Four), negative responses lead to negative ones, and positive responses to positive ones. Obviously, if this model is correct, it is advisable to try to break this cycle early. In order to do this, the early detection of developmental delay and parent–child interaction difficulties is essential.

Transactions. Another way to examine transactions is to study the extent to which environmental variables influence developmental change. We studied developmental change from one to three years in children in the following manner: *True negatives* were defined as children who were performing in the normal range at both one and three years, *false negatives* were defined as children who were delayed at three years but who had been functioning normally at one year, *true positives* were defined as children who were delayed at both one and three years, and *false positives* were defined as children who were delayed at one year but who were functioning normally at three years (Siegel, 1983).

The false positives had significantly higher scores on the HOME scale at one year than the true positives. That is, children who showed positive developmental change came from more stimulating environments as measured by the HOME scale than those who continued to show developmental delay. Conversely, the true negatives had significantly higher HOME scores than the false negatives. That is, children who showed significant decreases in developmental functioning had lower scores on the HOME scale at one year. These relationships are shown schematically in Figure 1.

In summary, despite very different early environments, differences between pre-term and full-term infants do not seem to persist through the early years. In this study, however, there was evidence that parents responded differently to delayed and non-delayed children, particularly later in development. Two trends were clearly evident in these data: The environments of delayed children are different from children who are developing normally; and children who are delayed early in development but who function normally later on have more stimulating homes than those who remain delayed, while children who are functioning normally in the early months but who are delayed later in development have less stimulating homes. These two trends suggest a transactional model (Sameroff and Chandler, 1975), in which environment and constitutional factors operate in an interactive fashion.

Developmental Disabilities and Their Influence on Interactions. The differences and similarities between children with difficulties and normal children may provide evidence for mutual adult and child influences on each other. We can determine whether children with developmental disabilities behave differently than normal children in social interactions. If parents and peers respond differently to these children than to normal children, we have a way to study the influences of child characteristics on the interaction. If the parents respond differently to children whose behavior is similar, we can infer that parental characteristics may be the determinants of the interaction.

90

Figure 1. Model of Some Transactional Effects

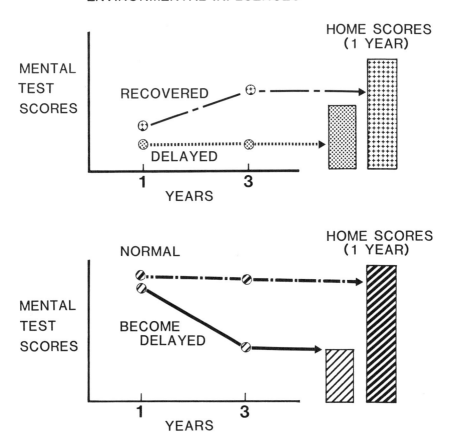

Interactions with Language-Delayed Children

We examined these relationships by studying the interactions of children with delayed language development with parents (for example, Cunningham and others, 1982) and peers (Siegel and others, 1983). Children with delayed language development were defined as having nonverbal intelligence scores on the Arthur Adaptation of the Leiter International Performance Scale that were no lower than one standard deviation below the mean for their chronological age and expressive and receptive age equivalent language scores on the Reynell Developmental Language Scales that were no more than 75 percent of their chronological age.

Interactions were videotaped in a playroom in which there were a variety of toys. The dyads (mother and child for the mother–child interaction study or two children for the peer study) were observed in a thirty-minute session consisting of fifteen minutes of free play and fifteen minutes of structured tasks. We observed normal and language-delayed children with their mothers and normal and language-delayed children interacting with an unfamiliar peer who was either normal or language-delayed.

Interactions were analyzed according to a modified version of the response-class matrix (Mash and others, 1973). Using a fifteen-second interval, the observer coded a child's response (command, command question, compliance, competing behavior, solitary play, question, interaction, or negative or no response) to specific antecedent behaviors of the mother or peer using the same code. Only one behavior from each child (or mother) was scored in each interval. Using the same response categories, a second observer simultaneously coded the mother or the second child's response to the antecedent behaviors of the first child, so that each participant in the interaction was viewed as an antecedent and a recipient in the interaction. This procedure allows the assessment of direction of effects. Coders were trained to a reliability level of at least 80 percent (cell-by-cell agreements over the total scores).

Parental Interactions. Language-delayed preschoolers engaged in fewer interactions with their mothers. On approximately 55 percent of the occasions when mothers of normal children were not interacting, their child initiated a verbal or nonverbal interaction. Language-delayed preschoolers, in contrast, initiated interaction on only 23 to 36 percent of these occasions.

Although language-delayed preschoolers displayed significantly less initiative than normal preschoolers during interactions with their mothers, their responsiveness to maternal interactions, questions, and commands did not differ. Bell and Harper (1977) have suggested two mechanisms based on a homeostatic control theory of interaction that parents might use in these situations. In an interactional situation, parents try to maintain a certain level of contact and control with the situation. They use the two mechanisms of upper-and lower-limit controls to keep the interaction at an optimal level. Upper-limit controls are designed to reduce excessive or inappropriate behavior, while lower-limit controls are designed to increase insufficient or nonexistent behavior. As predicted by Bell and Harper's (1977) formulation, the response of mothers to normal and language-delayed children was quite similar. The number of interactions initiated by mothers, the distribution of positive and controlling responses to the child's play activities, and positive responses to cooperative behavior did not differ significantly. Mothers were equally likely to initiate interaction, question and respond to their child during play, and respond to those interactions initiated by their child. The lack of social initiative displayed by language-delayed children, therefore, appears more closely related to individual characteristics rather than maternal interactional strategies.

Cohen and others (1978) reported more pronounced differences in the interactions of normal and language-delayed children with their mothers at twenty-one months of age than were observed in the older groups of children studied here. It is possible that the children in the study by Cohen and others were also generally delayed. Older language-delayed children in the present study proved more interactive and tended to be more responsive to questions than younger language-delayed children; many normal reciprocal patterns of social interaction appear to have emerged. These studies suggest a developmental improvement in the interactions of language-delayed children that should be examined in future longitudinal studies.

Peer Interactions. A similar pattern of interactions emerged during interactions between language-delayed children and normal peers. In addition, language-delayed children proved significantly less responsive to those interactions initiated by peers. Bell and Harper's (1977) formulation suggests that normal peers might reciprocate with lower-limit control strategies designed to increase the language-delayed child's social responsiveness. As anticipated, normal peers initiated more frequent interactions, interrupted the language-delayed child's solitary play sequences more frequently, and used a proportionately greater number of commands and negative responses in an attempt to dominate and control the interaction.

In summary, the social interactions of language-delayed children are, in many respects, comparable to those of normal children. Language-delayed children, however, show a pronounced pattern of social unassertiveness in a variety of settings, which may provide fewer opportunities for informal teaching exchanges with adults or other children. In addition, language-delayed children proved relatively unresponsive to the interactions of peers, which may be more difficult to comprehend that those of mothers. Normal peers responded with an increase in controlling responses that may compound the child's lack of social initiative. Factors responsible for the development of this pattern need to be considered in future studies and intervention efforts.

The patterns of increased attempts at dominance and control by the partner in the social interaction and reduced responsiveness of the target child have been noted in studies of parent–child interaction of children with a number of developmental disabilities, for example, deafness (Wedell-Monnig and Lumley, 1980), epilepsy (Ritchie, 1981), and hyperactivity (Cunningham and Barkley, 1979).

Because the developmentally handicapped child is less responsive, it becomes increasingly difficult for adults and other children to respond normally. As the difficulties become more severe, the parental or peer responses to the disability become more severe. Mothers of hyperactive or retarded children respond with more controlling behavior than the mothers of preschool language-delayed children. Perhaps the cycle can be broken with both early identification of delay and training of parents to deal with difficulties.

Interactions with Generally Delayed Children

In contrast to the response of mothers to children with delays in expressive or receptive language but normal nonverbal abilities, the response of mothers to children with delays in both language and nonverbal abilities differs substantially from those of normal control children. Using a similar observational setting and coding system, Cunningham and others (1981) found generally delayed preschoolers spent more time in solitary play, initiated fewer interactions, and responded less frequently to maternal interactions and questions. Mothers gave more commands, initiated fewer positive interactions, and were less likely to respond positively to the child's interactions, play activities, and cooperative behaviors.

A more detailed analysis of these interactions provides evidence concerning the impact of the child's response on a component of maternal conversational strategies that exerts an important influence on the child's language development. In speaking to young children, adults and older peers systematically reduce the complexity of their speech (Cunningham and others, 1981; Moerk, 1974, 1975, 1976, 1977; Phillips, 1973; Snow, 1972). This is one component of a complex of conversational adjustments and teaching strategies that include shifting the pitch of their voice, speaking more slowly, pausing more frequently, reducing the incidence of disfluency, expanding utterances, and correcting grammar, syntax, or vocabulary (Moerk, 1977).

It is important to note that mothers of both language-delayed and normal children reduced the complexity of their speech to a level consistent with the child's language comprehension skills (Cunningham and others, 1982). Many children with severely delayed language expression provide feedback by response to interactions, questions, and commands to mothers regarding their comprehension of her speech. However, mothers use speech of a complexity significantly above the child's capacity to imitate or produce language. This may result in lack of conversational interchange, contributing to the positive feedback loop or downward spiral effect.

The lack of social initiative on the part of the language-delayed child may reduce the opportunities for parent–child interactions and the lack of such conversational interchange may reduce the possibility for the child's language growth. This sequence is an illustration of the positive feedback loop that we described earlier. Although the complexity of maternal language is generally adjusted on the basis of the child's comprehension skills, the accuracy with which individual mothers calibrate their language differs considerably (Cunningham and others, 1981, 1982). Correlational analysis suggests that accurate calibration of language complexity is linked to feedback provided by the child as to the level of language that he or she alone can comprehend. If children initiated more frequent interaction, were more responsive to maternal interactions, and asked more questions, mothers adjusted their language more accurately (Cunningham and others, 1981, 1982).

The analysis presented above demonstrates the contribution of the developmentally delayed child to the calibration of maternal conversational strategies that may in turn influence language development. Additional evidence is derived from a longitudinal study of the social, cognitive, and academic development of language-delayed children that is now being completed in our laboratory. The interactions of mothers with their language-delayed preschoolers were videotaped during thirty minutes of free play and structured task settings and analyzed according to the modification of the response class matrix described above. The behavioral indexes derived from this analysis were correlated with changes in expression and comprehension scores on the Reynell Developmental Language Scales calculated over a six-month test/retest interval. Children who initiated frequent interaction, asked more questions, spent less time in solitary play, and proved more responsive to their mother's interactions, questions, and commands displayed greater gains in language expression scores. No correlations were observed between maternal behavior in the free play situation and subsequent gains in language development. In the task setting, however, the amount of interaction initiated by mothers and their responsiveness to the child's interactions predicted subsequent gains in expressive language development. Positive responses to compliance were correlated with gains in language comprehension scores.

Treatment Studies

The comparative studies of maternal interactions with normal, specifically language-delayed, and generally delayed and hyperactive children discussed above identify a major source of stress in the families of developmentally handicapped children. Comparative and correlational studies, however, failed to clarify the etiology of these patterns or the relative contribution of the mother and child to the interactions observed. Recent pharmacological studies with hyperactive children, in contrast, provide causal demonstrations of the effects of particular child behaviors on parental reponses (Barkley and Cunningham, 1979; Cunningham and Barkley, 1979). In double-blind placebo cross-over trials using observational settings and coding systems similar to those described above, hyperactive children on Ritalin showed significant reductions in activity level, engaged in more sustained quiet play, and proved more compliant with maternal directions. In response to these shifts in child behavior, mothers of hyperactive children gave fewer commands and were more likely to respond positively to the child's social interactions, play activities, and cooperative behavior. Recently completed studies in our laboratories have demonstrated a similar pattern of interactions between hyperactive children and normal peers. Dose-related improvements in activity level, sustained concentration, and academic performance in a simulated school setting are accompanied by a reciprocal decrease in the controlling and negative responses of normal peers (Cunningham and others, 1980).

The pharmacological studies reviewed above provide evidence as to the bidirectional influences operating in parent–child interactions. Overactive, inattentive, noncompliant children appear to elicit a pattern of upper-limit control strategies (Bell and Harper, 1977), characterized by an increase in commands and negative responses and a decrease in positive responses to social interactions, quiet play, and cooperative behavior. This pattern of parental responses may compound and perpetuate the child's behavioral difficulties (Barkley and Cunningham, 1979; Cunningham and Barkley, 1979).

A more controlled demonstration of the effects of the language-delayed child's behavior on maternal responses is provided in the context of a recently completed treatment study. A group of eighty-six language-delayed preschoolers were randomly assigned to either a classroom language program based on the approach described by Cooper and others (1978) or a parent-training group based on a modification approach described by Forehand and McMahon (1981). A matched group of children participated in community programs. Children were subgrouped into specifically delayed (I.Q. greater than 85 on the Leiter International Performance Scale), or generally delayed (I.Q. less than 85) (Leiter, 1973). Pre-test, post-test and eighteen month follow-up evaluations of language expression and comprehension, cognitive and preacademic performance, interactions with mothers, and behavior were completed. Treatment-related improvements in the behavior of language-delayed children participating in the classroom program and reciprocal shifts in maternal responses are of particular interest. Language-delayed children participating in the five-month classroom program, which focused specifically on increasing the frequency and complexity of the child's verbal interactions, showed both statistically and clinically significant increases in the number of interactions initiated during play with their mothers, a significant increase in the use of questions, and a significant increase in positive responses to maternal questions and interactions. With the exception of an increase in the compliance ratio of language-delayed children in the community control groups, no significant changes were noted in the behavior of language-delayed children participating in parent-training program or community control groups. Although not involved in a formal parent-training program, mothers of those children participating in the classroom program showed significant increases in positive interaction and decreases in commands during both free play and structured task settings. No significant changes were noted in the response of mothers in the community control group.

Conclusions

In Chapter Four, Mash suggests that families may be conceptualized as a series of subsystems, serving a number of specific functions within the family. The studies reviewed here have focused on the effects of different developmental disabilities on various functions of the mother–child subsystem.

The language-delayed child, for example, may instigate fewer of the conversational teaching exchanges that contribute to language and cognitive, social, and emotional development. The teaching, socialization, and emotional functions of the mother–child subsystem, therefore, may be disrupted. The overactive, inattentive, noncompliant behavior of the attention-deficit disordered child prompts parents and peers to resort to a series of increasingly directive upper-limit controls that may compound and perpetuate the child's behavioral difficulties. The behavioral control, socialization, and emotional functions of the mother–child dyad may consequently be impaired. Generally delayed children initiate fewer interactions, prove less responsive to their parents, and prompt a pattern of parental responses that may, once again, impair language and cognitive, social, and emotional development.

Future studies in our laboratories will focus on the interrelationships among different subsystems in the families of developmentally handicapped children. A recently completed cross-sectional developmental comparative study of the families of normal and attention-deficit disordered children, for example, demonstrates significantly higher scores on depression rating scales for mothers but not fathers, increases in the alcohol consumption of both fathers and mothers, and a disruption in relationships with extended family members.

Future treatment studies need to focus on the effects of intervention at different levels of the family system on both subsystem and overall family functioning. Several studies, for example, have demonstrated that parent training programs that improve child management strategies may prompt collateral improvements in other aspects of family functioning (Eyberg and Robinson, 1982; Karoly and Rosenthal, 1977).

In summary, language-delayed children are less likely to initiate interactions and are somewhat less responsive than normal children. They are particularly reluctant to interrupt the interactions of parents or peers or the solitary play of peers. Normal children and parents use a variety of strategies to elicit responsiveness. They show increased use of commands, and normal children increase attempts at dominance and control over delayed or atypical children. Child characteristics clearly have a significant effect on interaction patterns. Whether the children are developmentally delayed or have specific problems, such as in typical language development, the course of family interactions can be quite difficult.

References

Barkley, R. A., and Cunningham, C. E. "The Effects of Methylphenidate on the Mother-Child Interactions of Hyperactive Children." *Archives of General Psychiatry,* 1979, *36,* 201–208.
Bell, R. Q., and Harper, L. V. *Child Effects on Adults.* Hillsdale, N.J.: Erlbaum, 1977.
Bradley, R. H., and Caldwell, B. M. "Early Home Environment and Changes in Mental Test Performance in Children to Thirty-Six Months." *Developmental Psychology,* 1976, *12,* 93–97.

Cohen, S. E., Beckwith, L., and Parmelee, A. H. "Receptive Language Development in Pre-term Children as Related to Caregiver-Child Interaction." *Pediatrics,* 1978, *61,* 16-20.

Cooper, J., Moodley, M., and Reynell, J. *Helping Language Development.* London: Arnold, 1979.

Crawford, J. W. "Mother-Child Interaction in Premature and Full-term Infants." *Child Development,* 1982, *53,* 957-960.

Cunningham, C. E., and Barkley, R. A. "A Comparison of the Interactions of Hyperactive and Normal Children with Their Mothers in Free Play and Structured Task." *Child Development,* 1979, *50,* 217-224.

Cunningham, C. E., Reuler, E., Blackwell, J., and Deck, J. "Behavioral and Linguistic Developments in the Interactions of Normal and Retarded Children with Their Mothers." *Child Development,* 1981, *52,* 62-70.

Cunningham, C., Siegel, L. S., and Offord, D. "The Dose and Age-Related Effects of Methylphenidate on the Peer Interaction of Hyperactive Boys." In R. Millich (Ed.), *Peer Relations Among Hyperactive Children.* Symposium presented at the meeting of the American Psychological Association, Montreal, 1980.

Cunningham, C. E., Siegel, L. S., van der Spuy, H. I. J., Clark, M. L., and Bow, S. "The Behavioral and Linguistic Interactions of Specifically Language-Delayed and Normal Children with Their Mothers." Unpublished manuscript, McMaster University, 1982.

Eyberg, S., and Robinson, E. "Parent-Child Interaction Training: Effects on Family Functioning." *Journal of Clinical Child Psychology,* 1982, *11,* 130-137.

Field, T. M., Dempsey, J. R., and Shuman, H. H. "Developmental Follow-up of Pre- and Post-term Infants." In S. L. Friedman and M. Sigman (Eds.), *Pre-term Birth and Psychological Development.* New York: Academic Press, 1981.

Forehand, R., and McMahon, R. *Helping the Noncompliant Child: A Clinician's Guide to Parent Training.* New York: The Guilford Press, 1981.

Goldberg, S. "Prematurity: Effects on Parent-Infant Interaction." *Journal of Pediatric Psychology,* 1978, *3,* 137-144.

Hunt, J. V. "Predicting Intellectual Disorders in Childhood for Pre-term Infants with Birthweights Below 1501 Grams." In S. L. Friedman and M. Sigman (Eds.), *Pre-term Birth and Psychological Development.* New York: Academic Press, 1981.

Hunt, J. V. "Learning Disabilities in Children with Birthweights #1500 Grams." *Seminars in Perinatology,* 1982, *6,* 280-287.

Karoly, P., and Rosenthal, M. "Training Parents in Behavior Modification: Effects on Perception of Family Interaction and Decisions on Child Behavior." *Behavior Therapy,* 1977, *8,* 406-410.

Leiter, E. "A Study of the Effects of Subliminal Activation of Merging Fantasies in Differentiated and Non-Differentiated Schizophrenics." Doctoral thesis, New York University, 1973.

Mash, E. J., Terdal, L. G., and Anderson, K. "The Response-Class Matrix as a Procedure for Recording Parent-Child Interactions." *Journal of Consulting and Clinical Psychology,* 1973, *40,* 163-164.

Moerk, E. "Changes in Verbal Child-Mother Interactions with Increasing Language Skills of the Child." *Journal of Psycholinguistic Research,* 1974, *3,* 101-116.

Moerk, E. "Verbal Interactions Between Children and Their Mother During the Preschool Years." *Developmental Psychology,* 1975, *11,* 788-794.

Moerk, E. "Processes of Language Teaching and Training in Interactions of Mother-Child Dyads." *Child Development,* 1976, *47,* 1064-1078.

Moerk, E. *Pragmatic and Semantic Aspects of Early Language Development.* Baltimore: University Park Press, 1977.

Phillips, J. "Syntax and Vocabulary of Mother's Speech to Young Children: Age and Sex Comparisons." *Child Development,* 1973, *44,* 182-185.

98

Ritchie, K. "Research Note: Interaction in the Families of Epileptic Children." *Journal of Child Psychology and Psychiatry,* 1981, *22,* 65–71.

Rode, S. S., Chang, P., Fisch, R. O., and Sroufe, L. A. "Attachment Patterns of Infants Separated at Birth." *Developmental Psychology,* 1981, *17,* 188–191.

Sameroff, A. J., and Chandler, M. J. "Reproductive Risk and the Continuum of Caretaking Casuality." In F. D. Horowitz (Ed.), *Review of Child Development Research.* Chicago: University of Chicago Press, 1975.

Shattuck, D., Siegel, L. S., and Cunningham, C. E. "Mother-Child Interaction and Cognitive Development." Paper presented at the Society for Research in Child Development, Detroit, 1983.

Siegel, L. S. "Reproductive, Perinatal and Environmental Factors as Predictors of the Cognitive and Language Development of Pre-term Infants." *Child Development,* 1982a, *53,* 963–973.

Siegel, L. S. "Reproductive, Perinatal, and Environmental Variables as Predictors of Development of Pre-term (©1501 grams) and Full-term Children at Five Years." *Seminars in Perinatology,* 1982b, *6,* 274–279.

Siegel, L. S. "Early Cognitive and Environmental Correlates of Language Development at Four Years." *International Journal of Behavioral Development,* 1982c, *5,* 433–444.

Siegel, L. S. "Home Environmental Influences on Mental Development in Pre-term and Full-term Children in the First Five Years." In A. W. Gottfried (Ed.), *Home Environment and Early Mental Development.* New York: Academic Press, 1983.

Siegel, L. S., Saigal, S., Rosenbaum, P., Morton, R. A., Young, A., Berenbaum, S., and Stoskopf, B. "Predictors of Development in Pre-term and Full-term Infants: A Model for Detecting the At Risk Child." *Journal of Pediatric Psychology,* 1982, *7,* 135–148.

Siegel, L. S., Cunningham, C., and van der Spuy, H. I. J. "Interactions of Language-Delayed and Normal Preschool Boys with Their Peers." Unpublished manuscript, McMaster University, 1983.

Snow, C. "Mother's Speech to Children Learning Language." *Child Development,* 1972, *43,* 549–565.

Wedell-Monnig, J., and Lumley, J. M. "Child Deafness and Mother-Child Interaction," *Child Development,* 1980, *51,* 766–774.

Linda S. Siegel is professor of psychiatry at McMaster University and associate editor of Child Development. *Her research interests include learning disabilities and attentional deficits in children.*

Charles E. Cunningham is assistant professor of psychiatry at McMaster University. His research includes the study of hyperactive and language-delayed children.

Children characterized simultaneously by both aggression and withdrawal form a group particularly at risk for schizophrenia, and such behavioral vulnerability may reflect predisposing factors in the child.

Current Adjustment and Family Functioning of Children Behaviorally at Risk for Adult Schizophrenia

Jane E. Ledingham
Alex E. Schwartzman
Lisa A. Serbin

The high-risk methodology proposed by Mednick and McNeil (1968) involves the prospective, longitudinal study of individuals whose risk of psychopathology later in life exceeds the risk for the general population. As a method for gaining information relevant to the etiology of schizophrenia, it has several advantages over other approaches. Unlike investigations of the functioning of individuals who are already schizophrenic, the high-risk methodology yields information uncontaminated by the effects of confounding variables such as hospitalization, labels, and medication regimes. Furthermore, unlike retrospective records studies of children who later become schizophrenic, it

The findings reported in this chapter are based on work in progress as part of the Concordia Longitudinal High-Risk Project, supported by the Conseil Quebecois de Recherche Sociale, and the National Health Research and Development Program, Canada.

A. Doyle, D. Gold, D. S. Moskowitz (Eds.). *Children in Families Under Stress.*
New Directions for Child Development, no. 24. San Francisco: Jossey-Bass, June 1984.

provides information directly relevant to the hypothesis of interest to the investigator, information which may not be available from records produced many years previously.

Most high-risk studies (Anthony, 1972; Asarnow and others, 1978; Erlenmeyer-Kimling, 1978; Mednick and Schulsinger, 1970; Neale and Weintraub, 1975; Sameroff and others, 1982) have defined the child's risk for later schizophrenia in terms of parental characteristics. That is, they have all chosen to study children with at least one schizophrenic parent. The study of children of schizophrenics involves several implicit assumptions about how best to identify the child at risk and about the representativeness of schizophrenics with schizophrenic parents. These assumptions deserve close scrutiny.

Limitations of High-Risk Studies of the Children of Schizophrenics

Selecting parental variables to index child risk appears to imply that information about parents is more relevant to predictions about the children's later adjustment than information about the children themselves. Psychologists have traditionally assumed that children's influence on their parents is trivial in comparison with parental influences on the child. This unidirectional model interprets all evidence of a relationship between deviance in the family and psychopathology in the child as indicative of the contribution of the parents. However, recent work (Bell and Harper, 1977) suggests that children deserve considerable attention as determinants of parental behavior. Definitions of risk that make use of child characteristics do not have to make assumptions about a specific model of influence within the family, since child behavior can serve simultaneously as a postulated causal factor in its own right and as an indirect marker for parental influence. Moreover, information about children may prove to be more readily accessible and less subject to biases from factors such as social desirability response sets than information about parents. The study of the child's perceptions and attributions concerning family stressors may indeed prove to be more discriminating for predictive purposes and more meaningful than the nature of the stressors themselves. These considerations suggest that distinctive advantages exist for definitions of risk that specify characteristics of the child rather than of the parent.

The purpose of the high-risk design is to increase the probability of finding later schizophrenia in the children chosen for the study. The reason, of course, for the overwhelming adoption of the criterion of "having a schizophrenic parent" to denote risk, is that this criterion does reliably, as indicated by a long history of studies, increase the number of schizophrenics found in the sample being studied. We know that having one schizophrenic parent increases the risk for later schizophrenia from 1 percent to 12–15 percent, even for children removed from the schizophrenic parent very early in life by adoption (Heston, 1966). The risk for children with two schizophrenic parents is even greater: Approximately 35 to 50 percent later become schizophrenic. Other methods of identifying children at risk rely upon less definitive evidence to show that their criteria identify a greater number of schizophrenics in their sample than the 1 percent rate of schizophrenia found in the general population. For this reason, other methods of defining risk, although necessary, may appear less likely to succeed both to investigators and to granting agencies concerned with the cost/payoff ratio in underwriting expensive longitudinal studies. However, the generality of the results coming from studies of the children of schizophrenics may be limited. We know that only one schizophrenic in ten has a similarly diagnosed parent. Furthermore, schizophrenics with a family history of schizophrenia have been found to differ in several significant ways from schizophrenics with families clear of the disorder (Kinney and Jacobsen, 1978; Sedvall and Wode-Helgodt, 1980). The finding of differences in the symptomatology and course of schizophrenia as a function of the parents' psychiatric status suggests that defining risk in terms of parental diagnosis may provide information about only one very select subgroup of pre-schizophrenics.

Alternative Definitions of High Risk

The high-risk methodology has recently been invoked to study children vulnerable not only to schizophrenia but to a broad range of later problems of adjustment. Several investigators have begun studies of children for whom the elevated risk for later psychopathology is defined by characteristics of the child rather than by characteristics of the parent. The criteria for risk being used in these studies are numerous. They include selecting children on the basis of deviant autonomic responses (Mednick and others, 1975), deviant neurotransmitter levels (Coursey and others, 1980), social isolation (Rubin and Daniels-Beirness, 1983), high scatter in daily classwork performance (Blechman and others, 1981), cyclothymia (Depue and others, 1981), and multiple-criterion screens, including behavior ratings by teachers, peer ratings of isolation and rejection, poor reading achievement and high absenteeism (Kolvin and others, 1977). These developmental changes in the high-risk methodology as it enters its adolescence are laudable. However, while these studies can be expected to generate important information on the consequences of such characteristics, their claim to elevate the risk of the child for later psychopathology, despite their *a priori* appeal, is often weakened by the absence of evidence indicating that these are characteristics of moderate stability over time that have some predictive power.

Defining high risk in terms of disordered peer relations appears to provide a promising avenue, since there is well-documented evidence that measures of children's social behavior with peers are powerful predictors of vulnerability (Cowen and others, 1973; Rolf, 1972). Two fundamental factors that have emerged repeatedly from studies of deviant social behavior in children are aggression (also labelled as conduct problems, acting-out, or externalizing behavior) and withdrawal (often labelled as personality problems or over-controlled or internalized behavior). Agression, thus, is defined broadly here as a constellation that includes acting-out, physical agression, disruptiveness, and attention-seeking behaviors, while withdrawal refers to a pattern involving shyness, social isolation, and oversensitivity.

Despite substantial differences in the methodologies of investigations, reports of precursor patterns of aggression and withdrawal are found consistently throughout the literature on the characteristics of pre-schizophrenics. Retrospective records studies of teachers' comments about boys who later became schizophrenic have found that these pre-schizophrenics were described more often than control subjects as antisocial, negative, and disagreeable, and apathetic, passive, lacking in heterosexual contacts, and inactive in groups and sports (Bower and others, 1960). Results from follow-up studies of children who attended child guidance clinics have indicated that pre-schizophrenics were described more often than other clinic children as physically aggressive, delinquent, and as more alienated from and hostile to acquaintances (Robins, 1974). While shy, withdrawn behavior in childhood by itself has not been found to increase the risk of later psychopathology, aggressive symptomatology in childhood does. Morever, two retrospective follow-up studies of child guidance clinic populations indicate that children with a high degree of both antisocial and withdrawn symptoms produced a higher proportion (up to 11 percent of schizophrenics) than did any other group (Robins, 1979).

Early results from high-risk studies also characterize the pre-schizophrenic as both aggressive and withdrawn; Mednick and Schulsinger (1970) have reported that children of schizophrenic mothers were more often described by teachers as loners. Furthermore, those children at risk who later showed signs of psychiatric distress were rated as more disturbing to the class, more aggressive, and more domineering than were the children at risk who remained well.

These results and others suggest that aggression and withdrawal are implicated as patterns that characterize the behavior of the pre-schizophrenic. Nevertheless, it is not clear what the temporal relationship between these patterns is. Since most studies have combined descriptions of behavior across a large age range and since few studies have looked for the co-occurrence of these patterns in a given individual, it is not clear whether these patterns occur together in the life of the pre-schizophrenic or are mutually exclusive. Thus, it might be true that patterns of aggression and withdrawal represent distinct, stable, and mutually exclusive pathways to schizophrenia, perhaps leading to different subtypes of schizophrenia. Or it might be the case that aggression and withdrawal both occur in the life of the pre-schizophrenic, but sequentially. Finally, both aggression and withdrawal might occur simultaneously to form a pattern that characterizes the pre-schizophrenic. This line of reasoning suggests that a third, novel target group of children, characterized as simultaneously aggressive and withdrawn, should be identified for study in addition to aggressive targets and withdrawn targets.

The Concordia Project

The Concordia project began in 1976. It is a prospective, longitudinal investigation of children identified by their peers as highly aggressive, highly withdrawn, highly aggressive and withdrawn, or nondeviant. Peer ratings were selected as the vehicle for identifying target groups due to their ability to predict maladjustment in adulthood and demonstrated sensitivity to subtle differences in social adjustment during childhood (Hartup and others, 1967). For example, Rolf (1972) found that boys with schizophrenic mothers were not differentiated from controls by teachers' ratings, but were distinguished by peer sociometric measures. Furthermore, Mednick and Schulsinger (1970) have reported that peer relations succeeded in discriminating which high-risk children would later break down, while psychiatric ratings failed.

Following the identification by peers of target children, teacher and parent ratings of the behavior of these children were collected; home interviews were made to assess parental adjustment, marital satisfaction, and general family functioning; and the children were brought to the university for testing on measures previously found to discriminate between schizophrenics or pre-schizophrenics and controls. Three years following initial subject selection we carried out follow-up peer assessments that allowed us to determine the stability of these behavior patterns over time.

The Pupil Evaluation Inventory (PEI) developed by Pekarik and others (1976) was used as the peer-nomination instrument. It contains items that load on three orthogonal factors: aggression, withdrawal, and likeability. Each class was asked to nominate those boys or girls in the class who best fit the description of each item on the questionnaire. Boys and girls were rated separately by the class in different administrations so that, due to sex differences on these dimensions, we did not identify only male aggressive targets and only female withdrawn targets. Between November 1976 and February 1978 we administered the PEI to approximately 1100 children in grade one, 1300 children in grade four, and 1700 children in grade seven.

We chose to study only Quebec children whose first language was French, because French speakers are one of the most stable populations in North America: 1971 Census figures show that Montreal had the lowest outward-migration ratio of twenty metropolitan census areas in Canada. From 1966–1971 only 22 percent of French-speaking inhabitants moved and only 2 percent left the province. The low mobility of this population should minimize attrition rates as we follow our sample into adulthood.

From the 4100 children initially tested we selected our target children. The total number of nominations for each child was calculated separately for items loading on the aggression factor, the withdrawal factor, and the likeability factor, and these totals were standardized by conversion to Z scores within each class and sex to eliminate the effects of differences in class size and in rater standards across classrooms. Those children whose aggression Z scores exceeded the 95th percentile and whose withdrawal Z score fell below the 75th percentile were designated as aggressive targets. Similarly, the withdrawal Z scores for children designated as withdrawn fell in the top 5 percent of Z scores on withdrawal, and their aggression Z score fell below the 75th percentile. Aggressive-withdrawn target subjects were designated as those whose Z scores fell in the top twenty-five percent on both aggression and withdrawal. Control subjects were selected randomly from those whose Z scores fell below the 75 percentile for both aggression and withdrawal. The selection of these cut-off points resulted in the identification of a total of 183 aggressive subjects, 219 withdrawn subjects, and 251 aggressive-withdrawn subjects.

Peer Nominations. Choosing Z scores as our selection criteria allowed us to estimate what percentage of all children tested would fall into each of our target groups. We assumed that aggression and withdrawal were independent and therefore expected to identify about 4 percent of our total sample as aggressive, 4 percent as withdrawn, and about 6 percent of our total sample as aggressive-withdrawn targets. However, this was not the case. As grade level increased, the probability of identifying aggressive subjects and withdrawn subjects increased systematically, while the probability of identifying subjects who were both aggressive and withdrawn decreased. Thus, our assumption that aggression and withdrawal are orthogonal at all ages appears to be untenable. In grade one, aggression and withdrawal occurred together with greater frequency than the independent-dimensions assumption would predict: we identified more aggressive-withdrawn targets but fewer aggressive targets and fewer withdrawn targets than we had expected. However, in grade seven, the opposite was true: the co-occurrence of aggression and withdrawal was a much rarer event than we had anticipated, while both the number of aggressive targets and the number of withdrawn targets exceeded our expectations. It appears that there is a developmental trend for behavior to become more consistent as the child gets older, and that children who are both aggressive and withdrawn are behaviorally less mature.

We also obtained from the PEI a rating of likeability for each child. There was a highly significant classification by grade level interaction. This was due primarily to the systematically lower likeability scores for the aggressive-withdrawn group as grade level increased. The fall in the likeability scores in this group as grade level increased closely paralleled its decrease in frequency of identification. The lack of popularity for this group may reflect the fact that inconsistency or lack of predictability of behavior is aversive to peers because predictable behavior facilitates social interchange. It may also reflect the greater immaturity of this group.

Ratings by Teachers and Parents. Following the identification of our target sample and control group, teachers of these children were asked to rate the behavior of these children on the Devereux Elementary School Behavior Rating Scale (Spivack and Swift, 1967). These ratings served as a check on the validity of our selection procedures and as a means of collecting additional information about our target groups.

In general, the teacher ratings validated the results of our peer selection procedures. Aggressive and aggressive-withdrawn groups scored higher than the other two groups on scales related to aggression, that is, scales of classroom disturbance, impatience, disrespect-defiance, and external blame. As expected, the control group was fairly consistent along the normative means established for the instrument. However, the most striking result to emerge from the teacher-rating data pertains to the marked deviances of the aggressive-withdrawn group, who received ratings most deviant from established norms on ten out of fourteen scales. The aggressive-withdrawn group was evaluated as significantly more deviant than all other groups on the three scales, as more externally reliant, more inattentive-withdrawn, and as more unable to change from one activity to another.

Mothers' ratings indicated that target groups were behaving differently from controls not only in the school but also at home. Clearly, the deviance of our target groups is not specific to only one environment and is not a function solely of the biases of one type of rater. Again, as in the teacher ratings, the aggressive-withdrawn group was highly salient; they were rated highest on distractability, poor self-care, pathological use of the senses, and need for adult contact. These ratings suggest a certain immaturity about this group.

Laboratory Testing. Tasks chosen for the first round of laboratory testing included four subtests from the Wechsler Intelligence Scale for Children, the Lincoln-Oseretsky Motor Development Scale, and the Matching Familiar Figures test. They were designed in general to tap significant determinants of general competence that show marked developmental changes. Overall, there were surprisingly few differences between groups on cognitive measures. The aggressive-withdrawn group was clearly differentiated on the Lincoln-Oseretsky Scale: This group received significantly lower motor development scores than all other groups. This finding is in line with other reports that the pre-schizophrenic has deviant motor skills (Erlenmeyer-Kimling, 1978; Fish and Hagin, 1973) and is suggestive of an underlying neurological dysfunction in this group.

Three-Year Follow-up. Three years following the initial identification of target groups and controls, we collected follow-up peer assessments on all children who had remained in the same school system. Sixty-seven percent of the aggressive group, 68 percent of the withdrawn group, and 73 percent of the aggressive-withdrawn group were retrieved in this fashion. We are currently searching neighboring school boards to locate additional target subjects and reduce our attrition rates.

Since we had originally identified subjects in regular classes in grades one, four, and seven, we expected to find the overwhelming majority of these children in regular classes in grades four, seven, and ten. However, as we tracked our sample, we quickly realized that many of them had failed at least one grade, or had been placed in special education classes, and that school placement was directly related to subject classification. Aggressive and aggressive-withdrawn subjects had fared most poorly: Eighty-three percent of the control group were in regular classes at the expected grade level, as compared to 75 percent of withdrawn subjects, 59 percent of aggressive subjects, and 52 percent of aggressive-withdrawn subjects. While aggressive children and withdrawn children had an equal chance of failing or being placed in a special class at all grade levels, the proportion of subjects who failed or were in special clases increased with age for controls and for aggressive-withdrawn subjects. Moreover, the decline in success at school with age was more dramatic for the aggressive-withdrawn group. Rates of regular class placement at the expected grade level for the aggressive-withdrawn group were 63 percent for subjects originally identified in grade one, 45 percent for those in grade four, and 35 percent for those in grade seven, as compared to 92 percent, 83 percent, and 78 percent of the controls respectively. Finally, aggressive-withdrawn children appeared to have suffered multiple academic setbacks: More aggressive-withdrawn subjects had both failed a grade and been placed in a special class (12 percent) than subjects in any other group (aggressive 7 percent, withdrawn 2 percent, control 0 percent). Boys in all groups fared more poorly than girls. Insofar as the academic and social requirements of the school provide a good approximation to the occupational and interpersonal demands with which the adult must cope, these results point to the poorer early adaptation of aggressive and aggressive-withdrawn children. That rates of school failure and special class placement increased with grade level for aggressive-withdrawn subjects but not for aggressive subjects or withdrawn subjects suggests that for the former group there is a progressive deterioration over time. It is perhaps analogous to, or an early manifestation of, the "downward drift" in social status that is reported for many schizophrenics. The general finding that different kinds of children fall out of the mainstream of the educational system at different times may be one important determinant of discrepancies between cross-sectional and longitudinal findings (Gersten and others, 1976).

The differential academic success of target groups has important implications for our interpretations of retest data. Significantly more aggressive and aggressive-withdrawn children were retested in special classes that contained children very different from the children in regular classes who had initially identified target subjects. Because peer nominations require the rating of each child relative to his or her classmates, and because the composition of the comparison group for aggressive and aggressive-withdrawn subjects shifted to a more deviant group from initial testing to follow-up, it appears likely that absolute levels of aggression and withdrawal are underestimated by the scores these subjects received at follow-up. This is worth remembering in interpreting the data on the stability of classification from test to retest.

Withdrawn subjects were most likely to receive the same classification at follow-up: Thirty-four percent of this group retained the same label as opposed to 18 percent of aggressive targets and 21 percent of aggressive-withdrawn targets. While only 2 percent of withdrawn subjects and 6 percent of aggressive subjects were again identified as target subjects but were reclassified into different target groups, 17 percent of aggressive-withdrawn subjects were reclassified into a different target group at follow-up. This provides some longitudinal validation for our hypothesis that there is a developmental trend for inconsistent behavior patterns to become more consistent over time. In total then, 24 percent of the aggressive group, 36 percent of the withdrawn group, and 38 percent of the aggressive-withdrawn group received at follow-up a target classification reflective of continuing extreme deviance, according to some very rigorous criteria for stability.

What Is an Aggressive-Withdrawn Child? The phrase "aggressive-withdrawn," while it accurately describes the procedures used to select this group, probably does little to define the most salient features that distinguish this group from the other target groups. The identification-rate data, ratings by mothers, and the motor development scores suggest that they are an immature group. Teacher ratings and parent ratings suggest that they are a distractable group with attentional problems. Their peers rate them as less likeable than other children. Thus, a more complete characterization of the aggressive-withdrawn group should probably account for its uniqueness by making reference to its immaturity, attentional difficulties, or lack of popularity with peers.

We adopted two strategies to obtain a clearer picture of other ways in which this group differs from aggressive and withdrawn targets. The first was to perform discriminant analyses on the item scores of the Pupil Evaluation Inventory. We wanted to find out whether there were items that distinguished aggressive-withdrawn targets from aggressive targets and which ones characterized aggressive-withdrawn targets more than withdrawn targets. Separate analyses were carried out to contrast aggressive-withdrawn with aggressive and withdrawn groups respectively. These analyses indicated that aggressive-withdrawn subjects received more nominations than aggressive subjects on aggression items of "acting like a baby," "being mean and cruel to other children," "giving dirty looks," and "wanting to show off in front of the class"; they received fewer nominations on aggression items of "starting a fight over nothing" and "acting stuck up."

Aggressive-withdrawn subjects received more nominations than withdrawn subjects on withdrawal items of "never seeming to have a good time" and "being usually chosen last for group activities"; withdrawn subjects received more nominations for "being unhappy or sad." This apparent lack of affect, either positive or negative, suggests that the aggressive-withdrawn subject, like the schizophrenic, is anhedonic. It is also notable that the aggressive-withdrawn group was discriminated from both aggressive targets and withdrawn targets on two items; they received more nominations as "those who act like a baby" and "those who are usually chosen last to join in group activities." This reinforces findings from other sources that characterize this group as primarily immature and rejected by peers.

The second attempt to refine our conceptualization of the behavior of the aggressive-withdrawn child involved observing the actual behavior of this group in spontaneous peer interactions in the schoolyard. The pilot data suggest that while aggressive and withdrawn targets behave differently from control subjects, aggressive-withdrawn targets do not differ from control subjects in their behavior. They are, however, responded to differently by peers, receiving less attention and more attack. What has elicited these reactions will require further study.

In summary, aggressive-withdrawn children appear to be similar in many dimensions to the pre-schizophrenic. They represent a statistically infrequent event, at least at older ages, and are less likeable than their peers. There is also some evidence for developmental lags in motor development. The hypothesis that children who are both aggressive and withdrawn are highly deviant individuals is corroborated by teacher ratings and ratings by mothers.

In our study, teachers reported that the aggressive-withdrawn group was more distractable, more oblivious to what was going on in class, more dependent on and easily influenced by others, less able to change from one task to another, and slower to complete work than other target groups or controls. Mothers described this group as more distractable, more sensitive to incoming stimuli, tending to take poorer care of themselves, and needing more contact with adults than all other groups. These results support the interpretation that aggressive-withdrawn children are more immature than others. The decreasing probability of identifying aggressive-withdrawn children as age increases further suggests that this pattern of behavior is characteristic of a developmentally earlier, less mature mode of interaction than either aggression or withdrawal alone. The normal course of development appears to involve a tendency for patterns of aggressive and withdrawn behavior to become mutually exclusive as age increases. Older children lacking this consistency of behavior are perceived by peers as less socially skilled. The demonstrated lags in motor development illustrate that his immaturity in the aggressive-withdrawn child extends beyond the sphere of social functioning. That the aggressive-withdrawn group was described by teachers as more distractable than other groups takes on special significance in that one of the most widely accepted theories of schizophrenic deficit postulates a core attentional deficit.

Family Background. To obtain a global impression of family functioning, home visits were made and the parents completed the Locke-Wallace Marital Adjustment Test and a shortened version of the Minnesota Multiphasic Personality Inventory (Kincannon, 1968). In addition, a structured interview was used to collect information on the spouse's need for psychological treatment and contact with the police as reported by his or her partner, and on the financial resources of the family, family solidarity, and childrearing practices.

The relationship between disturbed family functioning and deviant child behavior is well established. In this sourcebook, the chapters by Mash, O'Leary, and Goldstein provide extensive discussions of the probable nature of this relationship. Additional evidence documents the significance of the early parent–child relationship for the child's later social success with peers (Easterbrooks and Lamb, 1979; Pastor, 1981). Research with primates suggests that even temporary, short-lived disruptions in the parent–child relationship produce detectible changes in the child's social interactions with peers (Suomi, 1979). Thus, peer relations appear to serve as a sensitive barometer for detecting disturbances within the family.

The causal model that highlights parental influences on children predicts that more disruption should be found in families of target children than in families of controls. Preliminary findings in the present study, however, were not consistent with this prediction. There were no differences between groups in parents' rates of contact with police, or need for psychological treatment as reported by the spouse. Neither fathers or mothers of any target groups were more likely than parents of control subjects to have a deviant MMPI profile. Target groups were no more likely to come from single-parent families than were control subjects and parents of target children in intact families did not report more problems in their marriages than parents of control subjects. There were also no significant differences between target and control groups in socioeconomic status. However, parents of aggressive and withdrawn children were more likely than parents of aggressive-withdrawn children and control subjects to report having financial problems ($X(3) = 8.02$, $p < .05$). The more serious financial difficulties of the former two groups are probably a consequence of the fact that they also had larger families (X (3) = 23.67, $p < .01$). Thirty-five percent of aggressive children and 41 percent of withdrawn children came from families with five or more children, compared to 18 percent of aggressive-withdrawn children and 8 percent of controls.

A number of inferences can be made concerning the relative absence of signs of disturbed functioning in the family data of the target children. One consequence of not beginning with a sample of disordered parents should be reduced rates of extreme parental deviance. It is possible, therefore, that the disturbances within these families were too subtle to be detected by instruments that deal with macro-measurements of family functioning. These considerations have prompted us to expand our family assessment procedures to include more subtle indexes of functioning such as family stressors, social supports available to family members, and concordance of perceptions and attributions of parent and child concerning family stresses. It is also possible that particular combinations of these and similar variables may interact to affect development of children.

Conclusions

Our oldest subjects are now leaving home and school. Their social and occupational success as young adults will serve as further markers of adjust-

110

ment. This oldest cohort is also approaching the period of risk for onset of schizophrenic symptomatology, and we will be devoting more attention to the detection of breakdown. Information about the adjustment of these subjects throughout their adult life will provide the ultimate criterion for evaluating our definition of risk.

Selecting for risk on the basis of child characteristics rather than those of the parents is a successful means of predicting adjustment. By using as a point of departure the phenomenon of interest, maladjustment in the child, child-centered risk studies make a minimum number of assumptions regarding precursors of deviance. Such a strategy provides a necessary point of comparison for evaluating the generality of studies that identify parental variables as the primary etiological factors for psychopathology. That is, most examinations of the family contexts of children's development begin with the family and, inferring from family data to child development, find significant patterns of relationships. Starting with children who are clearly labelled as deviant in a context apart from the family, we have worked back to trace family functioning and have found no readily identifiable indications of abnormal functioning in the family. This benign picture is maintained even though the aggressive-withdrawn child is also perceived as abnormal within the family context. We have emphasized the need for more refined measures of family functioning to more fully assess family influences on this pattern of social deviance in children, and such work is underway. Should these data replicate the absence of family pathology obtained to date, we will have to consider the possibility that some children's problems exist independently of problems in the family. The finding of deviance in children in a relatively normal context would suggest that for this pattern of disordered functioning, biological factors may provide a more compelling explanation than do environmental factors.

References

Anthony, E. J. "A Clinical and Experimental Study of High-Risk Children and Their Schizophrenic Parents." In H. R. Kaplan (Ed.), *Genetic Factors in Schizophrenia.* Springfield, Ill.: Thomas, 1972.

Asarnow, R., Steffy, R., MacCrimmon, D., and Cleghorn, J. "An Attentional Assessment of Foster Children at Risk for Schizophrenia." In L. Wynn, R. Cromwell, and S. Matthysse (Eds.), *The Nature of Schizophrenia.* New York: Wiley, 1978.

Bell, R. Q., and Harper, L. V. *Child Effects on Adults.* Hillsdale, N.J.: Erlbaum, 1977.

Blechman, E. A., Kotanchik, N. L., and Taylor, C. J. "Families and Schools Together: Early Behavioral Intervention with High-Risk Children." *Behavior Therapy,* 1981, *12,* 308–319.

Bower, E. M., Shellhammer, T. A., and Daily, J. M. "School Characteristics of Male Adolescents Who Later Became Schizophrenic." *American Journal of Orthopsychiatry,* 1960, *30,* 712–729.

Coursey, R. D., Buchsbaum, M. S., and Murphy, D. L. "Psychological Characteristics of Subjects Identified by Platelet MAO Activity and Evoked Potentials as Biologically at Risk for Psychopathology." *Journal of Abnormal Psychology,* 1980, *89,* 151–164.

Cowen, E. L., Pederson, A., Babigian, H., Izzo, L. D., and Trost, M. A. "Long-term Follow-up of Early Detected Vulnerable Children." *Journal of Consulting and Clinical Psychology,* 1973, *41,* 438–446.

Depue, R. A., Slater, F. F., Wolfstetter-Kausch, H., Klein, D., Gopolerud, E., and Farr, D. "A Behavioral Paradigm for Identifying Persons at Risk for Bipolar Depressive Disorder: A Conceptual Framework and Five Validational Studies." *Journal of Abnormal Psychology*, 1981, *90*, 381–437.

Easterbrooks, M. A., and Lamb, M. "The Relationship Between Quality of Infant-Mother Attachment and Infant Competence in Initial Encounters with Peers." *Child Development*, 1979, *50*, 380–387.

Erlenmeyer-Kimling, L. "A Program of Studies on Children at High Risk for Schizophrenia." In E. J. Anthony, C. Koupernik, and C. Chiland (Eds.), *The Child in His Family: Vulnerable Children.* New York: Wiley, 1978.

Fish, B., and Hagin, R. "Visual-Motor Disorders in Infants at Risk for Schizophrenia." *Archives of General Psychiatry*, 1973, *28*, 900–904.

Gersten, J. C., Langner, T. S., Eisenberg, J. C., Simcha-Fagan, O., and McCarthy, E. D. "Stability and Change in Types of Behavioral Disturbance of Children and Adolescents." *Journal of Abnormal Child Psychology*, 1976, *4*, 111–127.

Hartup, W. W., Glazer, J. A., and Charlesworth, R. "Peer Reinforcement and Sociometric Status." *Child Development*, 1967, *38*, 1017–1024.

Heston, L. L. "Psychiatric Disorders in Foster-Home-Reared Children of Schizophrenic Mothers." *British Journal of Psychiatry*, 1966, *112*, 819–825.

Kincannon, J. "Prediction of Standard MMPI Scale Scores from Seventy-One Items: The Mini-Mult." *Journal of Consulting and Clinical Psychology*, 1968, *32*, 319–325.

Kinney, D., and Jacobsen, B. "Environmental Factors in Schizophrenia: New Adoption Study Evidence." In L. Wynne, R. Cromwell, and S. Matthysse (Eds.), *The Nature of Schizophrenia.* New York: Wiley, 1978.

Kolvin, I., Garside, R. F., Nicol, H. R., Leitch, I. and MacMillan, A. "Screening Schoolchildren for High Risk of Emotional and Educational Disorder." *British Journal of Psychiatry*, 1977, *131*, 192–206.

Mednick, S., and McNeil, T. F. "Current Methodology in Research on the Etiology of Schizophrenia." *Psychological Bulletin*, 1968, *70*, 681–693.

Mednick, S., and Schulsinger, F. "Factors Related to Breakdown in Children at High Risk for Schizophrenia." In M. Roff and D. Ricks (Eds.), *Life History Research in Psychopathology.* Vol. 1. Minneapolis: University of Minnesota Press, 1970.

Mednick, S. A., Schulsinger, F., and Garfinkle, R. "Children at High Risk for Schizophrenia: Predisposing Factors and Intervention." In M. L. Kietzman, S. Sutton, and J. Zubin (Eds.), *Experimental Approaches to Psychopathology.* New York: Academic Press, 1975.

Neale, J. M., and Weintraub, S. "Children Vulnerable to Psychopathology: The Stony Brook High-Risk Project." *Journal of Abnormal Child Psychology*, 1975, *3*, 95–113.

Pastor, D. L. "The Quality of Mother-Infant Attachment and Its Relationship to Toddlers' Initial Sociability with Peers." *Developmental Psychology*, 1981, *17*, 326–335.

Pekarik, E. G., Prinz, R. J., Liebert, D. E., Weintraub, S., and Neale, J. M. "The Pupil Evaluation Inventory: A Sociometric Technique for Assessing Children's Social Behavior." *Journal of Abnormal Child Psychology*, 1976, *4*, 83–97.

Robins, L. N. *Deviant Children Grown Up.* Huntington, N.Y.: Krieger, 1974.

Robins, L. N. "Follow-up Studies." In H. C. Quay and J. S. Werry (Eds.), *Psychopathological Disorders of Childhood.* New York: Wiley, 1979.

Rolf, J. E. "The Social and Academic Competence of Children Vulnerable to Schizophrenia and Other Behavior Pathologies." *Journal of Abnormal Psychology*, 1972, *80*, 225–243.

Rubin, K. H., and Daniels-Beirness, T. *A Longitudinal Study of Sociometric Status in Early Childhood.* Paper presented at the 50th Anniversary Society Biennial Meeting of the Society for Research in Child Development, Detroit, April 1983.

Sameroff, A. J., Seifer, R., and Zax, M. "Early Development of Children at Risk for Emotional Disorder." *Monographs of the Society for Research in Child Development*, 1982, *47*(7).

112

Sedvall, G., and Wode-Helgod, B. "Aberrant Monoamine Metabolite Levels in CSF and Family History of Schizophrenia." *Archives of General Psychiatry*, 1980, *37*, 1113–1116.
Spivack, G. and Swift, M. *Devereux Elementary School Behavior Rating Scale Manual.* Devon, Penn.: Devereux Foundation, 1967.
Suomi, S. J. "Peers, Play, and Primary Prevention in Primates." In M. W. Kent and J. E. Rolf (Eds.), *Primary Prevention of Psychopathology.* Hanover, N.H.: University Press of New England, 1979.

Jane E. Ledingham is assistant professor of psychology at the Child Study Centre, University of Ottawa. Her research interests include the study of atypical children, children at risk for adult behavior disorders, and cognitive deficit in schizophrenia.

Alex E. Schwartzman is member of the Centre for Research in Human Development, professor of psychology at Concordia University, and director of the Concordia Longitudinal High-Risk Project. His research interests include the study of high-risk children, adult schizophrenia, and life-span changes in atypical populations.

Lisa A. Serbin is director of the Centre for Research in Human Development at Concordia University in Montreal, where she is also associate professor of psychology. Her research interests include the study of high-risk and atypical children and also the development of sex roles and sex differences.

Index

A

Abused children, 66, 72, 73–74, 76–77
Achenbach, T. M., 70, 71, 79–80
Adams, R. G., 31
Affective style (AS), and schizophrenia, 49, 53, 55, 60
Affective Style Index, 53
Aggression: concept of, 102; study of, 103–109
Aid for Dependent Children, 9
Alberta Mental Health Research Council, 65n
Alexander, J. F., 66, 73, 80
Al-Khayyal, M., 61
Allison, P. D., 67, 80
Amish, P. L., 83
Analogue studies, on stress, 13–14
Anderson, K., 82
Anspach, D. F., 27, 29
Anthony, E. J., 100, 110
Aragona, J. A., 66, 80
Asarnow, R., 100, 110

B

Babigian, H., 110
Baer, D. M., 43–44
Baker, B. L., 38, 45
Baker, L., 80
Baldwin, A. L., 14, 29
Baldwin, L. M., 81
Baltes, P. R., 17, 19, 29, 31
Barkley, R. A., 69, 75, 80, 81, 92, 94, 95, 96, 97
Barling, J., 43, 44
Bartko, J., 62
Baruch, D. W., 36, 44
Bates, J. E., 68, 69, 70, 72, 80, 92
Bayley Scales, 87–88
Beavers, W. R., 31, 73, 80
Becker's research, 35
Beckwith, L., 97
Bell, R. Q., 36, 44, 65, 67, 68, 74, 77, 80, 82, 91, 92, 95, 96, 100, 110
Berenbaum, S., 98
Berger, M., 46

Berkowitz, R., 61
Bernard, J., 21, 27, 29
Bijou's research, 35
Birley, J. L. T., 60
Bishop, D. S., 81
Blackwell, J., 97
Blechman, E. A., 101, 110
Block, J., 29, 80
Block, J. H., 25, 29, 72, 80
Blood, R. O., 65, 80
Bloom, B. L., 27, 29
Boersma, F. J., 66, 81
Bond, C. R., 41, 44
Boss, P., 22, 29
Bow, S., 97
Bower, E. M., 102, 110
Boyd, J. L., 61
Boys, and divorce, 24. *See also* Sex differences
Bradley, R. H., 86, 96
Brassard, J. A., 68, 81
Brief Psychiatric Rating Scale (BPRS), 56, 59
Brim, O., 17
Britton, R. S., 66, 80
Broderick, J. E., 38, 40, 45
Brody, G. H., 66, 80
Bronfenbrenner, U., 14, 17, 19–20, 30
Brown, C. H., 31
Brown, G. W., 47–48, 54, 60
Brown, P., 23, 30
Brunnquell, D., 77, 81
Buchsbaum, M. S., 110
Buckhalt, J. A., 66, 80
Buech, B. U., 32
Bugental, D. B., 68, 69, 80
Burr, W. F., 22, 30

C

Cadoret, R., 25, 30
Cain, C., 25, 30
Cairns, R. B., 16, 30, 67, 80
Caldwell, B. M., 86, 96
California at Los Angeles, University of, schizophrenia studies at, 48–49, 51, 54, 58

Camara, K. A. 22, 25, 26, 27, 28, 31
Camberwell Family Interview (CFI), 48, 54, 55
Cantor, N. L., 68, 70, 80
Cantwell, D. P., 66, 80
Caporeal, L., 80
Casto, R. F., 23, 32
Cauble, E. A., 31
Centre for Research in Human Development (CRHD), 2
Chadwick, O. F. D., 46
Chandler, M. J., 89, 98
Chang, P., 98
Chapman, J. W., 66, 81
Chapman, M., 32, 68, 69, 74, 75, 81
Charlesworth, R., 111
Cherlin, A., 18, 30
Child effects research, and problem children, 68–70
Children: and marital discord, 35–46; premature, 86–90; resilience in, 28–29; stress and coping by, 7–33. *See also* Children behaviorally at risk; Developmentally delayed children; Problem children
Children behaviorally at risk: for adult schizophrenia, analysis of, 99–112; aggression and withdrawal in, 103–109; aggressive-withdrawn, 107–108; alternative definitions of, 101–103; conclusions on, 109–110; family background of, 108–109; follow-up of, 105–107; high-risk studies of, 100–101; laboratory testing of, 105; peer ratings of, 101–102, 103, 104; teacher and parent ratings of, 104–105
Chiriboga, D. A., 21, 23, 30
Clark, D. B., 38, 45
Clark, M. L., 97
Cleghorn, J., 110
Cline, D. W., 32
Cochran, M. M., 68, 81
Cohen, S. E., 92, 97
Cohort effects, and stress, 18–19
Cole, S. B., 65, 81
Colletta, M. D., 27, 30
Comeau, J. K., 31
Communication: drift of, 52; schizophrenia related to, 47–62
Communication deviance (CD): interactional correlates of, 49–53; and nonverbal behavior, 53; and parental role sturcture, 50–52; and schizophrenia onset, 49, 60

Concordia Longitudinal High-Risk Project, 99n, 103–109
Concordia University, 2
Conseil Quebecois de Recherche Sociale, 99n
Cooper, J., 95, 97
Coping: in children and families, 7–33; concept of, 9; research on, 20–29; as transition experience, 20–21
Corneilson, A., 61
Coursey, R. D., 101, 110
Cowen, E. L., 101, 110
Cox, M., 31
Cox, R., 31
Crawford, J. W., 86, 97
Crichton, L., 81
Cummings, C., 83
Cunningham, C. E., 2, 69, 75, 81, 85–98
Curley, A. D., 43, 45
Cutler, L., 21, 23, 30

D

Daily, J. M., 110
Daniels-Beirness, T., 101, 110
Day, R., 54, 59, 60
DeBlois, C. S., 83
Deck, J., 97
Deinard, A., 81
Dempsey, J. R., 97
Denmark, schizophrenia studies in, 54
Depue, R. A., 101, 110
Developmental status, and stress, 23–25
Developmentally delayed children: analysis of interactions by, 85–98; conclusions on, 95–96; environment and transactions of, 89–90; future research on, 96; with general delay, 93–94; and influence on interactions, 89; with language delay, 90–92, 95; parental interactions with, 91–92; peer interactions with, 92; and positive feedback loop, 88–89; premature, 86–90; as problem children, 66, 76; treatment studies of, 94–95
Devereux Elementary School Behavior Rating Scale, 105
Deykin, E., 73, 81
Direct observation, on stress, 13–16
Divorce, and stress, 12–13, 18, 24. *See also* Marital discord
Doane, J. A., 47n, 48–49, 55, 57, 61, 70, 81

Doleys, D., 42, 45
Douglas, V. I., 73, 81
Doyle, A., 1-3
Duffy, M., 27, 30
Dumas, J., E., 68, 74, 83
Dunn, J., 10, 30, 65, 81
During, S., 65n

E

Easterbrooks, M. A., 109, 111
Easterlin, R. A., 19, 30
Ecological approach, to stress, 19-20
Edelbrock, C. S., 71, 79-80
Egeland, B., 74, 77, 81
Eisenberg, J. C., 111
Elder, G. H., Jr., 17, 18, 19, 30
Emery, R. E., 25, 26, 30, 35n, 37, 41, 42, 43, 45, 66, 82
Endicott, J., 83
Ensminger, M. A., 31
Epstein, N., 26, 30
Epstein, N. B., 68, 73, 81
Erlenmeyer-Kimling, L., 100, 105, 111
Expressed emotion (EE): and construct validity issues, 54-55, 56, 57; cross-cultural validity of, 58-60; and parent characteristics, 57-58; and patient characteristics, 55-57, 58; replication studies on, 54; and schizophrenia, 47-48, 54-60
Eyberg, S. M., 66, 80, 96, 97

F

Falloon, I. R. H., 47n, 55, 58, 59, 61, 62
Families: of children behaviorally at risk, 108-109; disturbed, studying, 68-74; effects of atypical children on, 63-112; marital discord and parental psychopathology in, 5-62; with problem children, 65-84; resilience in, 28-29; resources of, and stress, 26-27; and schizophrenia course, 54-60; and schizophrenia onset, 48-53; social context of, 1; stress and coping in, 7-33
Family affect, schizophrenia related to, 47-62
Family systems theory: and problem children, 67-68; and stress, 11-12
Farr, D. 111
Feiring, C., 82
Field, T. M., 86, 97

Fincham, F., 45
Finnegan, D., 30
Fisch, R. O., 98
Fish, B., 105, 111
Fisher, L., 61
Fleck, S., 61
Forehand, R., 81, 95, 97
Fox, J. J., 73, 83
Frank, G. H., 70, 81
Freeman, W., 62
Furstenberg, F. F., Jr., 9, 27, 30

G

Garfinkle, R., 111
Garmezy, N., 29, 30, 48, 61
Garner, A. M., 66, 81
Garside, R. F., 111
Gelfand, D. M., 68, 80
George, L., 22, 30
Gerhardt, V., 22, 30
Gersten, J. C., 106, 111
Girls, and marital discord, 42, 44. See also Sex differences
Glazer, J. A., 111
Gold, D., 1-3
Goldberg, K. E., 80
Goldberg, L., 62
Goldberg, S., 86, 97
Goldstein, M. J., 2, 47-72, 109
Gopolerud, E., 111
Gore, S., 20, 27, 30
Gorham, D. R., 56, 61
Gossett, J. T., 31
Gottman, J. M., 15-16, 22, 30, 35-36, 45, 67, 74, 81
Graham, P., 46
Granvold, D. K., 23, 30
Great Britain, schizophrenia studies in, 47-48, 54
Griest, D. L., 66, 81
Gurman, A. S., 68, 81
Gythell, D., 30

H

Hagin, R., 105, 111
Haley, J., 68, 81
Hampe, G., 27, 32
Harburg, E., 30
Harper, L. V., 65, 67, 68, 74, 80, 91, 92, 95, 96, 100, 110
Hartup, W. W., 103, 111
Haynes, S. N., 70, 81

Health and Welfare Canada, 65*n*
Hendricks, A. F. C. J., 37, 46
Hess, R. D., 22, 25, 26, 27, 28, 31
Heston, L. L., 100, 111
Hetherington, E. M., 1-2, 7-33, 35, 41, 44, 65, 70, 81, 89
Hinde, R. A., 73, 74, 81
Hobbs, D. F., 65, 81
Home Observation for Measurement of the Environment (HOME), 86-88, 89
Howard, A., 22, 31
Hughes, H. M., 70, 81
Hultsch, D. F., 23, 31
Hunt, J. V., 86, 97
Hyperactive children, problems of, 66, 69, 71, 72, 73, 75-76, 77-78, 94-95

I

India, schizophrenia studies in, 54, 59
Interactions, social: analysis of, 85-98; with generally delayed children, 93-94; influence on, 89; with language-delayed children, 90-92; parental, 91-92; peer, 92; and prematurity, 86-90
Izzo, L. D., 110

J

Jacob, T., 70, 81
Jacobsen, B., 101, 111
James, J. E., 61
Johnson, S. B., 35, 45
Johnson, S. B., 38, 45, 72, 82
Johnston, C., 65*n*, 66, 69, 74, 75, 76, 77, 78, 82
Jones, J. E., 49, 51, 57, 71
Jones, S., 62
Jouriles, E., 35*n*
Joy, C. B., 31

K

Kagan, J., 17
Karno, J., 58-59, 61
Karoly, P., 96, 97
Kellam, S. G., 27, 31
Keller, B. B., 68, 82
Kelly, J. B., 12-13, 23, 24-25, 27, 28, 32
Kendrick, C., 10, 30, 65, 81
Kent, R. W., 37, 45
Kety, S. S., 62
Killam Resident Fellowship, 65*n*
Kimmel, D. C., 40, 45

Kincannon, J., 108, 111
Kinney, D., 101, 111
Kitson, C. G., 22, 27, 31
Klein, D., 111
Kniskern, D. P., 68, 81
Kolvin, I., 101, 111
Komarovsky, M., 18, 31
Kotanchik, N. L., 110
Kovitz, K., 82
Kramer, D. A., 32
Kuiper, L., 61

L

Labouvie, G. V., 32
Lader, M., 61
Lamb, M., 68, 74, 82, 83, 109, 111
Langner, T. S., 111
Le Programme de Formation de Chercheurs et d'Action Concertée, 2
Ledingham, J. E., 2, 99-112
Lee, C. L., 72, 82
Leff, J. P., 47-48, 54, 55, 59, 61-62
Leitch, I., 111
Leiter, E., 95, 97
Leiter International Performance Scale, 90, 95
Leober, R., 83
Lerner, R. M., 36, 45
Lester, G., 12, 31
Levin, S., 81
Levinger, G., 21, 31
Lewis, J. M., 17, 31, 47*n*, 50-53, 61
Lewis, M., 68, 74, 78, 82
Liberman, R. P., 62
Lidz, T., 51, 61, 62
Lieber, D. J., 50, 61
Liebert, D. E., 111
Life-span approaches, to stress, 17-19
Liker, J. K., 67, 80
Lincoln-Oseretsky Motor Development Scale, 105
Lobitz, C. K., 39, 45, 72, 82
Locke, H. J., 39, 45
Locke-Wallace Marital Adjustment Test, 39, 40, 108
Loney, J., 71, 82
Lumley, J. M., 92, 98

M

McCarthy, E. D., 111
McCarthy Scales of Children's Abilities, 87-88

MacCrimmon, D., 110
McCubbin, H. I., 11, 12, 22, 31
McDermott, J. F., 25, 31
McGill, C. W., 61
McMahon, R., 95, 97
McMahon, R. J., 81
MacMillan, A., 111
McNeil, T. F., 99, 111
McPherson, S. R., 61
Manela, R., 23, 30
March of Dimes Birth Defects Foundation, 85n
Margolin, G., 36, 45
Marital discord: analysis of, 35–46; and childhood problems, 36–39; in clinic samples, 39–41; effects of, 5–62; in nonclinic samples, 41–44; research needed on, 42–43
Markmann, H., 45
Martin, B., 65, 70, 81
Mash, E. J., 2, 65–84, 85, 89, 91, 95, 97, 109
Mason, P. R., 31
Matching Familiar Figures Test, 105
Matthews, K. A., 68, 82
Maughan, B., 32
Mednick, S., 99, 100, 101, 102, 103, 111
Messe, L. A., 83
Miklowitz, D. J., 47n, 55–57, 61
Minnesota Multiphasic Personality Inventory (MMPI), 108, 109
Minuckin, S., 68, 73, 82
Moerk, E., 93, 97
Moir, R. N., 31
Moodley, M., 97
Moos, B. S., 73, 82
Moos, R. H., 73, 82
Morrison, A., 29, 80
Mortimore, P., 32
Morton, R. A., 98
Moscowitz, D. S., 1–3
Moss, H. B., 61
Mothers, language calibration by, 86, 93–94. See also Parents
Mulhern, R. K., 68, 70, 82
Murphy, D. L., 110

N

National Health Research and Development Program, Canada, 99n
National Institute of Mental Health, 47n
Navran, L., 40, 45
Neale, J. M., 100, 111

Needle, R. H., 31
Nesselroade, J. R., 19, 29, 31
Nicol, H. R., 111
Normative and non-normative life events, and stress, 17–18
Notarius, C., 45

O

Offord, D., 97
O'Leary, K. D., 2, 25, 26, 30, 31, 35–46, 66, 82, 109
Olson, D. H., 22, 31, 73, 83
Oltmann's research, 38
Ontario Mental Health Foundation, 85n
Ouston, J., 32
Overall, J. E., 56, 61

P

Pais, J. S., 23, 31
Parent Adolescent Naturalistic Interaction Code (PANIC), 15
Parents: characteristics of, and expressed emotion, 57–58; children rated by, 104–105; developmentally delayed children in interaction with, 91–92; perceptions of problem children by, 69, 70, 72, 74–75, 77; role structure of, and communication, 50–52; self-esteem of, 78. See also Marital discord
Parke, R. D., 68, 74, 77, 83
Parmelee, A. H., 97
Passman, R. H., 68, 70, 82
Pastor, D. L., 109, 111
Patterson, G. R., 15, 31, 35, 37, 45, 65, 66, 68, 69, 74, 83
Patterson, J. M., 22, 31
Paykel, E. S., 10, 31
Pederson, A., 110
Pedler, L. M., 30
Peers: children rated by, 101–102, 103, 104; developmentally delayed children in interaction with, 92; as support in stress, 27–28
Pekarik, E. G., 103, 111
Perry, L., 30
Personality, and stress, 22–23
Peterson, D. R., 40, 46
Peterson-Quay Behavior Problem Check List, 40, 42
Pettit, G. S., 69, 80
Phillips, J., 93, 97

Phillips, J. S., 71, 83
Phillips, V. A., 31
Phipps-Yonas, S., 81
Plemons, J. K., 23, 31
Pless, I. B., 73, 83
Porter, B., 26, 31, 35n, 41, 42, 46
Prematurity, and social interactions, 86–90
Prinz, R. J., 111
Problem children: abused, 66, 72, 73–74, 76–77; analysis of, 65–84; and assessment issues, 70–74; background on, 65–66; and causality direction, 66–67; and child effects research, 68–70; and conceptual issues, 66–68; developmentally delayed, 66, 76, 85–98; effects of, 63–112; and family systems theory, 67–68; hyperactive, 66, 69, 71, 72, 73, 75–76, 77–78, 94–95; normal children compared with, 70; parental perceptions of, 69, 70, 72, 74–75, 77; studying 68–74; summary on, 79
Psychiatry, and stress, 11–13
Psychology, and stress, 13–17
Pupil Evaluation Inventory (PEI), 103, 104

Q

Quay, N. C., 40, 46
Quinton, D., 46

R

Rachman, S. J., 28–29, 32
Radke-Yarrow, M., 15, 32
Raicevic, H., 2
Raschke, H. J., 22, 31
Rausch, H. L., 69, 74, 83
Ray, R. S., 71, 83
Reese, H. W., 29
Reid, J. B., 37, 45, 46, 68, 74, 83
Reiss, D., 11, 32
Research Diagnostic Criteria, 71
Resilience, to stress, 28–29
Reuler, E., 97
Revealed Differences Task, 70
Reynell, J., 97
Reynell Developmental Language Scales, 90, 94
Ricci, J., 62
Richardson, M. S., 65, 83
Riley, M., 17
Ringland, J. T., 67, 74, 81

Ritchie, K., 92, 98
Ritzler, B., 61
Robins, E., 83
Robins, L. N., 102, 111
Robinson, E., 96, 97
Rode, S. S., 87, 98
Rodnick, E. H., 61
Rohrbeck, C. A., 83
Rolf, J. E., 101, 103, 111
Rosenbaum, A., 43, 46
Rosenbaum, P., 98
Rosenthal, D., 49, 61, 62
Rosenthal, M., 96, 97
Rosman, B., 62
Routh, D. K., 65, 83
Rowlands, O., 46
Rubin, K. H., 101, 111
Russell, C. S., 31, 83
Rutherford, R. B., 80
Rutter, M., 10, 16, 23, 25, 26, 28, 32, 39, 41, 43, 46, 80

S

Saigal, S., 98
Sameroff, A. J., 89, 98, 100, 111
Samios, M., 35n
Sarason, I. G., 22, 32
Satterwhite, B., 73, 83
Sawin, D. B., 68, 83
Scanzoni, J., 21, 32
Schaie, K., 19, 32
Schellie, S. G., 30
Schizophrenia: adult, children behaviorally at risk for, 99–112; aggression and withdrawal as precursors of, 102–103; analysis of family functioning and, 47–62; background on, 47–48; conclusion on, 60; course of, and family factors, 54–60; and expressed emotion, 47–48, 54–60; high-risk studies of children of, 100–101; onset of, and family factors, 48–53
Schools, as support in stress, 27–28
Schulsinger, F., 100, 102, 103, 111
Schwartzman, A. E., 2, 99–112
Sedvall, G., 101, 112
Seifer, R., 111
Self-reports, on stress, 13
Selye, H., 8, 32
Serbin, L. A., 2, 37, 99–112
Sex differences: and marital discord, 39, 40–41, 42, 43, 44; and stress, 25–26
Shanas, E., 27, 32

Shapiro, L., 62
Shattuck, D., 87, 98
Shellhammer, T. A., 110
Shennum, W. A., 80
Shuman, H. H., 97
Siegel, L. S., 2, 85-98
Simcha-Fagan, O., 111
Singer, M. T., 48, 49, 57, 61, 62
Slater, F. F., 111
Smith, A., 32
Snow, C., 93, 98
Social Sciences and Humanities Research
  Council of Canada, 2
Sociology, and stress, 11-13
South Africa, marital discord and child-
  hood problems in, 43
Southern California, University of,
  schizophrenia studies at, 55
Spanier, G. B., 23, 32, 36, 45
Spicer, J., 27, 32
Spitzer, R. L., 71, 83
Spivack, G., 105, 112
Sprenkle, D. H., 31, 83
Sroufe, L. A., 98
Stanford-Binet, 87-88
Steffy, R., 110
Stephenson, G., 83
Stevens-Long, J., 70, 83
Stinnett, N., 67, 70, 83
Stollak, G. E., 83
Stoneman, Z., 66, 80
Stoskopf, B., 98
Strang, J. S., 61
Stress: and affect, 10; analysis of, 7-33;
  background on, 7-8; concept of, 1, 8-
  9; conclusion on, 29; and developmental status, 23-25; dimensions of,
  9-10; and divorce, 12-13, 18, 24; ecological approach to, 19-20; from exits
  and entrances, 9-10; family resources
  and support systems and, 26-27; life-
  span approaches to, 17-19; multiple
  methods for, 16-17; multiple sources
  of, 10; perceptions and expectations
  in, 21-22; personal resources and
  characteristics and, 22-26; and problem children, 66; psychological approach to, 13-17; research on, 20-29;
  resilience to, 28-29; sociological and
  psychiatric approaches to, 11-13; and
  temperament and personality, 22-23;
  theoretical approaches to, 10-20; as
  transition experience, 20-21
Stewart, M. A., 66, 83

Strodtbeck, F. L., 11, 32, 49, 61,
  70, 83
Sturgeon, D., 55, 61
Suomi, S., 67, 83
Support systems: extrafamilial, 27-28;
  and family resources, 26-27
Synder, K. S., 62
Swift, M., 105, 112
Swift, W. J., 32

T

Taplin, P. S., 83
Tarrier, N., 54-55, 61
Taylor, C. J., 110
Temperament, and stress, 22-23
Terdal, L. G., 71, 82
Tessman, L. H., 24, 32
Teyber, E. C., 68, 70, 83
Thematic Apperception Test (TAT), 49
Toohey, M. L., 62
Trost, M. A., 110
Turkewitz, H., 40, 45, 46
Turner, J. T., 31
Turpin, G., 61
Twentyman, C. T., 77, 83

U

UCLA Social Attainment Scale, 56, 58

V

van der Spuy, H. I. J., 97, 98
Van der veen, F., 40, 45
Vaughn, C. E., 47-48, 54, 55, 58, 59,
  61-62
Venters, M., 22, 32
Vincent, J., 40, 46

W

Wahler, R. G., 66, 68, 73, 74, 83
Waisbren, S. E., 66, 83
Waldron, H., 65, 83
Wallace, K. M., 39, 45
Wallerstein, J. S., 12-13, 23, 24-25, 27,
  28, 32
Walsh, F., 69, 83
Walters, J., 67, 70, 83
Wechsler Intelligence Scale for Chil-
  dren, 105
Wedell-Monnig, J., 92, 98

Weinberg, S. L., 65, 83
Weinraut, M., 82
Weintraub, S., 100, 111
Weiss, R., 21, 22, 23, 25, 32
Wells, K. C., 81
Wenar, G., 66, 81
Wender, P. H., 49, 62
West, K. L., 61
Westman, J. D., 25, 32
White, D., 2
Whitehead, L., 43, 46
Wilcox, J. A., 36, 44
Wild, C., 57, 62
Wing, J. F., 60
Withdrawal: concept of, 102; study of, 103–109
Wode-Helgodt, B., 101, 112

Wolfe, D. M., 65, 80
Wolfstetter-Kausch, H., 111
Wolkind, W., 26, 32
Wood, D. D., 80
World Health Organization, 59
Wynne, L. C., 48, 49, 57, 61, 62

Y

Young, A., 98
Yule, B., 46
Yule, W., 46

Z

Zahn-Waxler, C., 32
Zax, M., 111